side walks

side walks

side walks

one woman's 30-year journey
to discover her roots and
find her way home

by julie dieterich pappas

side walks

dedication

To David, Noah & Nathanael ...
pass the story on.

To my family:
Gary, Johanna & Laura

To the three sisters:
Martha, Emma & Amelia

Emma, Martha, Amelia

What people are saying about
side walks

"From the very first page, I felt immediately drawn into Pappas' story — swept up in the rich sense of history and the deeply personal journey of her childhood. ... Her story felt like a mirror in places, and a window in others—quietly powerful and beautifully told." — Heather J.

"What a delightful journey these Side Walks are; a unique treasure hunt that yields gem after gem along the pathway of beautiful storytelling, well drawn experiences and authentic emotion. Julie's kind style invites the reader in and then envelops them in a world both familiar and specific. ... The book asks us to consider why we remember what we remember and dares us to consider what we've forgotten." — David B.

"Side walks led me to historically rich places that were completely new to me, and places that were heartbreakingly familiar. ... As she uncovers long-held family secrets, confronts mental illness in her own life, and shares the burden and beauty of putting a broken marriage back together, Julie invites us into a story that is both painfully personal and profoundly universal. — Dawn S.

"Side Walks is intensely personal but also wide-ranging. ... The stories told reveal the connections between generations and communities, and make the reader reflect on the paths that connect their own life to the lives of others. — Kim N.

"Julie Pappas has written a masterwork of memory, inheritance, and identity. ... Her voice is tender and fierce, honoring the ache of what was unsaid in past generations while bravely bringing those truths to light." — Missy A.

"Side Walks is an intimate journey through Northern Michigan exploring the author's genealogy, illuminating the ties that bind, seamlessly connecting, past, present and future." — Jennifer V.

contents

part 1: summer
up north 11
fossils 21
upon the land 23
to aunt martha's home 33
exploring the homestead 46
in the library 59

part 2: autumn
to the city 71
home 88

part 3: winter
to the doctor 105

part 4: spring
through the gate 113
back in time 121
little boys 127
to dad's workshop 128
the artist 133
into hiding 140
to uncle arnold's home 145
summer at the dieterich farm 147

Part 5: summer returns
back up north 153
two women 157
another way 169
into the chapel 172
into a garden 178

side walks

sidewalks

She grew up in a neighborhood with sidewalks
Cement squares linked with lines.
By the time she was 7, she could
Jump from one line to the next,
With a satisfying leap.

These squares served as a palette
For sidewalk chalk,
As a lane for bowling,
As a storefront for a painted rock business.
They took her around the block,
Around 4 blocks to a friend's house,
Around 8 blocks to the community swimming pool.

She could pull her yellow wagon with ease
Making a rhythmic beat with each line.
Some squares were cracked or didn't match up
Perfectly one to another,
Creating a disruption that threw her song off beat.
She could count how many squares it took
To go from her house to the stop sign,
And that never changed.

When the girls who lived 11 and 17 squares
Down the street cut her down with insults,
Tears clouded her vision,
But the sidewalk led her home.

Once in a while, she'd see someone's initials
In the cement block,
And hoped to have the chance to do the same,
To claim a 3' x 3' piece of property for herself .

Sidewalks ordered her suburban life
Like dot-to-dot lines
As she traced her way through childhood.

One day, she stepped off the sidewalk.

side walks

part 1
summer

*But the most astonishing thing about trees is how social they are.
The trees in a forest care for each other, sometimes even going so far
as to nourish the stump of a felled tree for centuries after it was cut
down by feeding it sugars and other nutrients and so keeping it alive.*
— Peter Wohlleben[1]

up north

It was late afternoon. The sun cast long shadows on the rows of gravestones appearing to march forward as time moved backward. Some gravestones stood erect, pristine, and were easy to read; others sunk into the ground or tumbled forward like old men from decades of nature's beating. I walked back to the forest's edge, crunching skeletal acorns with each step. I read unfamiliar names, not sure what I was looking for, but felt something; like a seed had been planted here. My eyes were drawn to a weathered stone, under the shadow of an elderly oak tree. It was off to the side; separate from most. It was curious. I was curious. Squatting down, I traced the name with my index finger.

Christena Dieterich, 1860-1892. My grandmother's maiden name was Dieterich. Could Christena be a relative?

[1]Wohlleben, Peter. The Hidden Life of Trees. Random House, 2015.

Dave and I had been on our way back to the family cottage in Indian River after a picnic in Harbor Springs, when on a whim or an ancestor's whisper, I spontaneously yelled, "Go straight!"

Dave, whose Hebrew name means *beloved,* turned off the turn signal, and instead of turning right on M-68, accommodated my impulse and continued straight along US-31 toward Brutus. I intently stared out the window trying to resurrect memories from childhood.

Other than the Brutus Camp Deli sandwich shop and post office the size of a hot dog stand to the left, and the non-descript Maple River Town Hall and gas station on the right, there seemed no reason to stop in this northern Michigan town. At Brutus Road, not sure which way to turn, we chose west, drove past a few tar-paper sided houses and soon found a modest white Mennonite church and cemetery on the north side of the road.

Dave had tentatively pulled up on the grass; there was no parking lot or driveway. "Dave, I found a Dieterich! Dave! Quick, come look!" I shouted as if the stone would vanish. He had been peering in the windows of the locked church building, so he jumped off an old cinder block and ran over to examine the artifact I was kneeling before.

"Who was she?" he asked. "I wonder why she was buried here, alone."

"I don't know, but I'm going to find out. This... is so... cool!"

I was gripped by the realization that this woman, who had died at the age of 31, had a story to tell. Here from the marker of death, I was feeling a breath of new life.

As a child, once a year my family left the sidewalks of our suburban Lathrup Village neighborhood to travel Up North, to northern Michigan. My dad, Gary, whose old Norse name means *spear or sharp wit,* loved the Petoskey area, having traveled there regularly as a child. Camping was the most frugal option, and I didn't mind. Trailblazing in the woods and sand dunes captured my innate desire to explore and discover nature's treasures. I could fashion a fort or create a network of nooks in an imaginary world of my own where I made my own rules, trying out an evolving independence.

Mennonite Church and Cemetery, Brutus, Michigan
Photos by Nate Pappas

Waking up at 4:00 AM with a push from Mom, Laura and I crawled into the backseat of Dad's teal blue 1970 Plymouth Fury for our annual vacation to the Petoskey State Park. There was no stopping Gary C. Hilpert. In order to get the best spot for camping, we had to arrive earlier than the early birds. The sun rose two hours later, half way there, waking us with aching stomachs.

"Mom, what's for breakfast?" I whined.

"Good morning, Sunshine!" she exclaimed, much too loud for my sleepy brain. "We'll stop at a rest-area to have cereal. I bought those mini-boxes you like." My sister cheered, I sneered. I had hoped to stop at McDonald's. My mom, Johanna, whose Germanic name means *God is gracious,* created a positive vibe in our family, even when challenges arose. Even when I was the cause of those challenges.

As the analog clock on the dashboard of the car turned to 9 AM, we ascended the last hill on US-31, catching a stunning view of the expansive periwinkle waters beyond the grassy, daisy-spotted dunes. "There she is! Beautiful Lake Michigan!" Dad announced as if he'd forgotten all the stress of home and work and travelling. I loved hearing Dad express this rare untainted joy. It made me happy too.

We descended into Petoskey past the hospital and strip malls into the quaint downtown. Transported to 1890 when Victorian storefronts first welcomed resorters, or *fudgies* as they are commonly called by the locals, we had arrived, but only for a second. Dad was on a mission and needed to get through the ever-increasing traffic moving east. The car jerked forward, jolting from one stop to the next. Dad huffed with agitation, as if we should be the only tourists in this tourist town. I turned up the volume on my Walkman to quell the swelling anxiety. When Dad was stressed, I was too.

Laura, whose Latin name means *victory,* piped up, "Look! There's the Indian Hills Gallery!" It was a sure sign of our close proximity.

I poked out from my invisible shell, "Hey! We have to go there so I can make a new bracelet!" The store had changed over the years, from a little shack to a splendid wooden art gallery with angled windows reflecting the sky above.

"Girls, we're almost to the campground! We can do all the things you want to do, later! Let's focus on getting settled in." Mom was good at redirecting our attention to the task at hand, though I was annoyed. This was our pattern.

Arriving at the entrance to the campground, we had to wait in a long line of cars to reserve the campsite. My legs bounced incessantly, partly because of needing to stretch, partly because of nerves. You never knew when Dad's fragile happiness would crack into irritation. Thankfully, Dad's plan to leave early paid off, and we landed in a large spot on the outer rim of the campground, sheltered under balsam, northern cedar and birch trees. This was Dad's version of a 5-star hotel room. But this was better. This was our favorite Up North landing spot; It was as familiar as home.

Once the car rolled into place, Laura and I jumped out with a flurry of plans. Dad and Mom painstakingly set up the massive two-room blue canvas army tent — much larger, heavier, and far more unwieldy than contemporary counterparts. Dad slipped out more than a few swear words in the process, as Mom did her best to accommodate his instructions, to appease his demands. Laura and I knew to stay out of their way, and searched for chipmunks to entertain us. Oddly, once the tent was set, the car unloaded, and sleeping bags in place, Dad disappeared to placate his own child-like obsession. He would leave us to take photos of old buildings, to replicate in his basement train exhibit. Creative passions were a diversion from obsessive thoughts often inhibiting his ability to unwind.

The barrage of seagulls crying out, "Ow! Ow!" sounded like angry cats, but reminded me of the beach on the other side of the dunes.

"Mom, can we go swimming after you're done making lunch? Please?" I begged while slapping on some shiny pink lip gloss.

Mom waved as my dad pulled away, exhaust tainting the air, then turned back to spread peanut butter on another slice of bread. "Sure thing," she answered distantly. "That's the plan after we clean up and get suntan lotion on!" Mom was beautiful. Even in her camping clothes, she had a preppy all-American vibe with her blue and white striped sea-style shirt and a sweater draped over her shoulders. I was a bit more on the wild side, experimental and artsy. Mom called it my costuming years.

Finally we were ready to go; I grabbed the Walkman and a towel. The three of us made our way out of the camping area, to the beach as quickly as possible over the sunbaked sand dune trail.

"Stay on the path, girls," Mom warned, "Look out for poison ivy!"

A painful memory stabbed the scars on the right side of my abdomen, visible between the top and bottom of my bikini bathing suit.

"I know, Mom!' I replied with a snarky tone. "How could I forget?"

We dropped off our stuff at an uncongested area closer to the dunes. Little kids played at the water's edge. I was no longer a little kid. As I took off my cover-up, I couldn't help but glance down at my small breasts. I flushed remembering the humiliation of a locker-room experience when it dawned on me, "I am the last girl to get a bra." But I did have a cool spiky haircut and long slender legs; I was fifteen and feeling like fledging the protective nest.

Running to the water's edge I challenged Laura, "I dare you to be the first to put your head under the water."

She didn't bite, "No, I dare YOU!" We ran into the lake, careful not to slip on the rocks covering the lake floor as we pumped our legs through the waves. When we got waist deep in the icy water, I called to Laura, "OK, let's do it together! Ready? 1, 2, 3!"

Under we went. Lake Michigan punched us in the gut. It was exhilarating torture. We swam, freer and colder than at the heated swim club pool back home. And when we could take it no more, we galloped back out to wrap ourselves in the beach towels Mom had just laid out, laughing as our teeth chattered.

"Afraid of a little cold?" Mom taunted with a twinkle in her eyes.

I situated my body on the wet towel with arms extended for optimal sun and turned on *Suzanne Vega*. Laura laid next to me. Glancing out of the corner of my eyes, I noticed she was maturing faster than me, even though she was 20 months younger. She was gorgeous with her swim team tan and blueberry eyes. Unbeknownst to me, she was being bullied at school because of her feminine figure. We girls can't win.

Petoskey State Park Photos by Laura Isaacs

© G. Randall Goss – USA TODAY NETWORK via Imagn Images

SISTERS Julie (left) and Laura Hilpert of Southfield are two attractions at Petoskey State Park.
(Graphic photo by G. Randall Goss) Printed in The Graphic, Thursday, Aug. 28, 1986

Mom only stayed about an hour, leaving to return to the campsite to take a nap and get dinner ready. No sooner had she left, two older boys approached, asking if we would meet them at a park across the street. Too shy to say yes, and too naïve to sense danger, I suggested, "Maybe tomorrow."

A reporter came to take photos of beach goers for the local paper, *The Graphic,* and captured us posing. While I felt chosen, as if I was the prettiest on the beach that day, I felt awkward and unprepared for attention from the opposite sex. I suggested to Laura we make our way back through the dunes to the campsite. She agreed.

Dad returned once the sloppy joes were ready; not a moment too soon. We all sat together at the picnic table covered by a red and white checked tablecloth, worn with a few holes. Dad talked about his escapades. We listened. This was a common routine for dinner table conversation.

At sunset we headed back to the beach and walked along the water's edge as a family. Dad loved Lake Michigan sunsets. Joy in his eyes reflected the warm light; for a moment he smiled toward the horizon. Tonight I was in search of Petoskey stones: fossilized coral with a unique floral pattern. I longed to find my own; to experience the joy I'd caught in Dad's eyes when he lifted the once rough, now smooth ancient stone out of the water. I walked with my head turned downward, neck stiff. Though the sun was setting, and the air cooled drastically, I was determined not to leave until finding my own stone, a bit of place to take back to my suburban home hundreds of miles away.

Back at the site, Dad started a fire and we sat on camp stools listening as he shared stories about childhoods spent in these familiar forests and dunes. We didn't live here, but Dad, in his way, was communicating that we were from here. Of here. These intimations soaked into my skin like the heat of the beach sun. Wistfully, Dad spoke of his northern relatives: of his mother Emma, born in a farmhouse not far from where we sat; of Carl her older brother who ran the farm bossing the cows around (calling them bastards); of Aunt Martha, the first in the Dieterich family to own a car. I was mildly interested in these tales and imagined how different it was to grow up on a farm. I missed Grandma Emma who had passed away 2 years previous. But we didn't talk about that. This was a time for stories. Not feelings.

Dad put out the fire at 10:00 PM and reminded us of our scheduled visit with Aunt Martha the next day. I rolled my eyes. "But Dad, I want to go to the beach! Can't a girl just relax and go swimming on her vacation?" I remembered the boys who might meet us at the park.

Dad chastised me with *the family is important* lecture and I took off to brush my teeth at the public restroom. I washed the lip gloss off and looked at my reflection. Without it, I looked like a child. I didn't like being told what to do, but I wrestled with wanting to please my parents. Either way, I really didn't understand why we had to visit Aunt Martha on just the second day of our vacation. There were far more interesting things for me to do.

Sinking into my sleeping bag, I tried to get comfortable atop the roots and stones beneath the tent floor. I felt awkward, caught somewhere between childhood innocence and teenage angst. But somehow the smell of balsam fir trees and the sound of distant waves wafting over the dunes calmed my busy mind and anxious body, lulling me to sleep.

side walks

fossils

A million shiny stones under my vulnerable feet,
I dance with the rhythm of the playful waves,
Scouring the water's edge for a treasure, a Petoskey stone.
Dad says, "You can see them when they are wet."
"But Dad," I complain,
"There are a million shiny stones under my vulnerable feet!"

Mother sized footprints under my independent feet,
I bend down scooping handfuls of stones,
Some sharp, scraping my palms, some smooth, easing the pain.
Mom says, "Don't lose heart, treasures take time to find."
"Ok Mom," I doubt,
I follow Mother sized footprints under my independent feet."

Glowing earthen colors under my tired feet,
I glance up at the setting sun,
Clouds darkening with brushstrokes of purple, orange and pink,
I demand, "I must find one before the sun goes down."
Mom says, "There is always tomorrow."
Tears fall upon glowing earthen colors under my tired feet.

Icy cold waves under my numbing feet,
Like death that overtakes the warmth of a soul,
I lean down and pick up a floral-patterned gray stone and ask,
"Dad, is this a Petoskey stone?" He smiles.
I wrap my fingers tightly around proof of a bygone era,
With icy cold waves under my numbing feet.

Grains upon grains of chilling sand
Under my resilient feet
I make my way on the dark forest path,
To a shelter,
Where I tuck my treasure away,
In remembrance.

side walks

upon the land

Identifying a Petoskey stone was a childhood marvel; to find the name of a family member engraved on a tombstone felt like an adult equivalent. The day after Dave and I had explored Brutus, I got up early to make my way to the Emmet County Courthouse in Petoskey. With a legal-pad, a bag of snacks and coffee-to-go from Jesperson's, I was prepared to begin a full-on excavation of my family's history. Our two-week vacation became a mad pursuit to find as much as possible about a story I knew little about. To start, I'd search for the death record of Christena Dieterich.

Dressed in tan stretch pants, an oversized white sweatshirt and pink flip-flop sandals, I felt out of place entering the formal and formidable building. I had no idea where to start, so I gingerly asked a guard where the records were kept. He kindly advised me to start at the Clerk's Office, on the second floor.

My flip-flops slapped the terrazzo floor with every step and echoed down the empty disinfectant-smelling halls. I tentatively pushed open a heavy glass door, emblazoned with the words *County Clerk* on the pane, just above eye level. Upon hearing my entrance, the no-nonsense clerk with long, straight blonde hair unhurriedly turned from her computer screen to ask, "May I help you?" It was obvious I was an intrusion.

I stuttered, "Um, yes. Uh. How would I go about finding a death record from 1892?"

"Right this way. But you'll have to leave your coffee at the front desk. No food or drinks allowed." I thought, *of course, silly me!*

She took me into a smaller, dimly lit room with rows and rows of musty records on metal shelving units. She pulled out a large, heavy book and said, "You should find what you are looking for here; but remember, names are not always spelled correctly. When you are finished, you can pay for an official record."

"Thank you, I appreciate your help," I replied. She scurried back to her work, leaving a waft of fruity perfume in her wake (not my type). I sat at a small wooden table on a metal shop stool and opened the first page of the Emmet County death records.

The yellowed paper, faded ink and old-style handwriting made the records hard to read, so when I ultimately found the record of Christena's death, I let

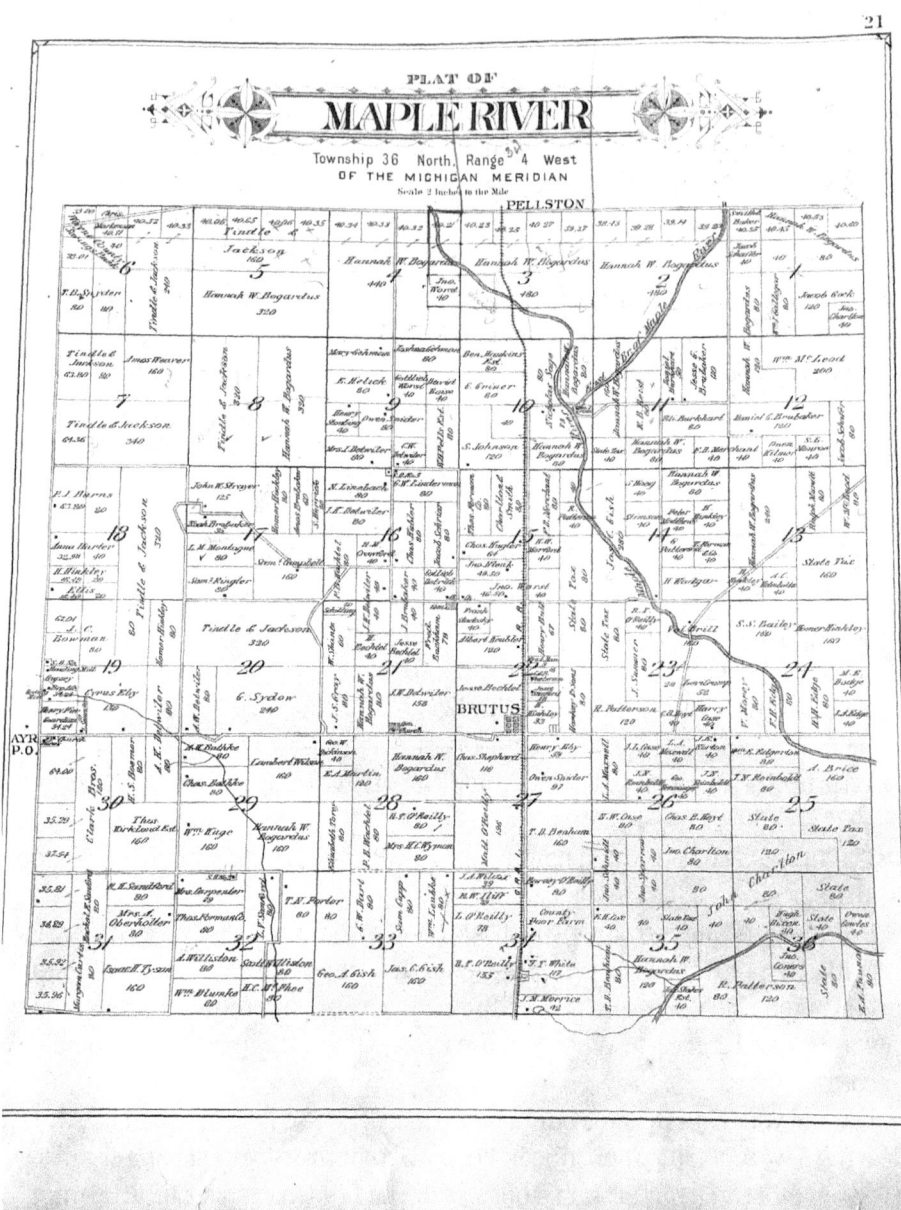

From the Plat Book of Emmet County Michigan, The Consolidated Pub. Co.

out an audible gasp. It was like peering into a portal to the past.

The record said that Christena Dieterich died at the age of 31 of dropsy. The technical diagnosis of dropsy is *edema,* when the body swells as a result of abnormal amounts of fluid in the body's tissues, caused by congestive heart failure, liver failure, kidney failure and/or malnutrition.[2] I envisioned the scene: her husband and children gathered around her bed, candles lit, flickering silhouettes on log walls. A rural doctor arriving on horseback, treated the illness by drawing out fluid, knowing that his efforts would likely be in vain.

Dropsy would have been a death sentence for Christena. She was a young mother, children in need of her nurturing presence and guidance. An unthinkable tragedy; and so very far from her parents in Germany.

Who was this woman? Had I found my people? I said out loud, "I need to find my great-grandfather's grave."

Leaping off the stool, I bounced over to the office clerk to ask if there was a map of Emmet County that would show where graveyards were located.

"Just a moment please..." she finished a joke with a co-worker and then directed, "Right this way," flinging her hair over her shoulder.

The clerk gently placed the *Plat Book of Emmet County Michigan, The Consolidated Pub. Co. 1902* on the table and warned, "If you'd like a copy, I'll need to handle the document myself."

"Absolutely!" I assured her.

The plat maps were the size of poster boards, but not nearly as sturdy. Turning to the *Plat of Maple River,* I could see blocks of land labeled with family names, divided by roads and rivers. I had never looked at a book like this before and I was enthusiastic about the newness of the experience and the oldness of the book. My eyes were adjusting to the fine-print. I identified another cemetery, located just north of Brutus on Red School Road; but my heart skipped a beat when I noticed my great-grandfather's name Gotlieb Detrick (actual spelling- Gottlieb Dieterich). In Section 16, just across the street from the cemetery, he was listed as the owner of 40 acres of land in 1902.

I had found my people.

---

[2]Estes, J. Worth. VIII.39- Dropsy from Part VIII Major Human Diseases Past and Present. Cambridge University Press, 2008. https://www.cambridge.org/core/books/abs/cambridge-world-history-of-human-disease/dropsy/C58BF7044399EE1E911299B54E39E484

Zion Evangelical Church *Photos by Laura Isaacs*

I politely requested a copy, packed up my belongings, and returned to the cottage to ask Dave if he would go with me back to Brutus. This was too momentous to experience alone and there was no one I wanted to share the joy of discovery with more than Dave. He was my best friend.

———————

The windows were down in our little Honda Civic, the air conditioning having broken years before. Dave was driving fast and down shifted as we passed through the remnants of Brutus.

"Slow down! Here it is! Turn here! Red School Road!" I stammered, panicked we would miss it.

Rather than seeing a red school, in the distance I spotted a white clapboard church on the right, and a small-fenced cemetery on the left. These had been key ingredients to my recent discoveries; I was hopeful it would be true again. Dave parked haphazardly on the shoulder of the road; I sprang out of the car into a grassy ditch, tripped on a stone, breathed in a swarm of dust, and coughed. "This is it, Dave!" I looked at him, noticing his eyes were on me, enjoying me and this moment together. He kissed me, warm and tender, and patted my butt.

"Where do we start?" he asked with a cheeky grin. I placed my hand on his cheek, kissed him once more, and replied, "Remember making love at that park along Lake Michigan?" I winked at him. "We could explore the possibilities...but later."

A flock of yellow warblers spying on us, alit from a row of spruce. Taken aback, I exclaimed, "Aren't they beautiful?" Dave was still looking at me, and replied, "Yes she is." I blushed and turned to open the back door of the car, where a file held a copy of the Maple River Plat. Back to business. Shielding my sensitive blue eyes from the sun, I tried to pinpoint the location of the Dieterich property.

I glanced across the street and pointed, "According to the map, Gottlieb's home would have been situated on the corner of Kugler and Red School Road, adjacent to that church in the abandoned field." I sighed with disappointment; there was no physical structure on the land, just one lonely apple tree. Its branches barely produced leaves, let alone apples,

Site of Dieterich property on Red School Road, Maple River Township, Michigan Photo by Nate Pappas

with twisted bare branches that looked to be a hundred years old. *A hundred years old.*

I moved toward the tree, imagining children's voices celebrating the juicy red apples, but as I reached out to touch the ragged bark, I realized the tree appeared grief-stricken, fruitless. I thanked her for providing nourishment to my family.

Turning away, I searched for remnants of a foundation, walking through waist-high grasses and swatting bugs off my thighs. There was no sign of a stone fireplace, no outline of a cabin floor, no remaining logs or fences, nothing. I wondered, *could I find a photo to give more evidence than a tiny square on a century-old map?* I stood transfixed on the land. There was no home here, but this was home.

I knelt down and scooped the sandy soil, letting it slip through the cracks between my fingers, pondering the people who made a life for themselves here, planting crops and eating the nutrients of the soil. Looking up, the property stretched to a tree line of red pine, maybe 80 acres deep. I was in awe as I reflected on the elements below my feet that nourished the flesh and bones of my ancestors. Of me.

I considered how my parents had faithfully provided for our basic needs. Though Dad was frugal and going out to eat was a rarity, I never worried whether food would be on the table. We were dependent on Mom and Dad's jobs and their resourcefulness. But the Dieterich's fashioned a home out of trees and grew or raised what they ate, completely dependent on the land. This was a vastly different lifestyle from the one I had known.

We turned to cross the street, and entered the Maple River Township Cemetery. I surveyed the names: *Wurst, Schreier, Klenk, Kuebler, Kugler.* Occasionally I would sweep off some old grass clippings or a fallen tree branch in order to decipher the names etched on stones. After 10 minutes or so, I spied a small gravestone in a corner of the cemetery enveloped by orange daylilies and tall grasses. I tenderly pushed them aside and read the name. *Magdalena Dieterich, Mother.*

"Mother!" I said out loud. "This must be my great-grandmother." Dave ran to my side. Behind Magdalena, a smaller gravestone, without the floral display, read *Gottlieb Dieterich, Father.*

Dave reacted, "Oh my. Here they all are!" And he was right. Next to

Maple River Cemetery, Michigan Photos by Nate Pappas

Magdalena and Gottlieb, we saw *Harriet and John Dieterich, Children,* engraved on a large stone. Indeed, I had found my people. My family of origin. This cemetery, this ground on which I stood, once supported the grieving Dieterich family, one loss after another. My heart raced; my mind buzzed.

I thought; *graveyards don't hold all the secrets.* I still have living relatives! Though Grandma Emma had passed when I was 13, I could still talk to her sisters: Aunt Martha, born in 1901, who lived nearby in Petoskey, and Aunt Amelia, lovingly known as Aunt Mitzy, born in 1914, who lived in Detroit.

"Dave, we could visit Aunt Martha, and ask her all about this!" Dave was enjoying the ride nearly as much as I was, and eagerly agreed.

"Give her a call!" he encouraged. I said good-bye to this family I longed to know and we headed back to the cottage, full of wonder.

Dave and I picked up the tradition my father had begun years ago of regular visits with Aunt Martha. I'd never had to make the phone call before, and frankly, I barely knew this elderly aunt; but I was not to be deterred.

Before I dialed her phone number, I warned Dave and his parents to move outside so I could speak loud enough. Aunt Martha was hard-of-hearing and wore hearing aids that were less-than-exemplary, shall we say.

"HELLO? AUNT MARTHA?" I waited, "THIS IS JULIE."

"Who?"

"JULIE!"

"Julie?"

"YES, JULIE, GARY'S DAUGHTER."

My mother-in-law quietly opened the screen from the deck, reached in and closed the door-wall. She would later tease that I was yelling so loud I might not have even needed the phone. *Funny, Eunice.*

"Gary's daughter?"

"YES!"

"Oh. Hello." Her aged voice squeaked through the handset.

"I'M IN TOWN AND WOULD LIKE TO VISIT YOU!" I could hear Dave and his parents chuckling on the deck outside.

She replied with her soft crackled voice, "Why don't you come for dinner? I'll make some soup."

"WE'D LOVE TO!" My yelling this time was from excitement; I'll own that one. We made a date for the next evening, Saturday, at 5:30 PM. I scribbled her address down on an old Ken's Village Market receipt and yelled my goodbye into the telephone. I flung the glass door wall and the screen door open and burst onto the deck.

"We're going for dinner tomorrow!" I exclaimed.

My father-in-law, Ed, smiled wryly and said, "We heard."

to aunt martha's home

Taking the step to visit Martha felt like a responsible thing to do. Like something my dad would do. Dad was faithful to his relatives; he even visited Aunt Martha on his honeymoon to Petoskey with my mother. As the story of my family's history was beginning to take on shape and form, I felt confident that Dad would approve of my effort. I wondered why he hadn't shared more openly about his childhood, or his mother's childhood for that matter. I needed to know more, to uncover possible secrets that may have impacted Dad's world, and therefore mine, for better, or for worse.

On our way to Aunt Martha's apartment, Dave and I stopped at the Emmet County Courthouse to obtain death records of the family members I'd found at the Maple River Township Cemetery. These records of their death would prove, ironically, that they had lived.

It was 4:00 PM when we arrived. I got out of the car and attempted to press the wrinkles out of my floral skirt. This time I was dressed appropriately for the occasion, with a pair of classy tan heels; no flip-flops in sight.

"May I help you?" the clerk asked, as if never having met before.

"I'm in need of some official death certificates, please." I smiled, tossed some curls behind my shoulder, and straightened up, as if I were a force to reckon with. "Early 1900s."

Dave prodded, "Give her the names!"

I dropped the façade, "Oh yes, um, here are the names of the records I am looking for. Thank you!"

Dave politely excused himself to sit and read while I went to work.

I handed the clerk a handwritten list with the dates I'd recorded from the gravestones: *Gottlieb Dieterich-1922, Magdalena Dieterich-1925, John Dieterich-1905, and Harriet Dieterich-1920.*

Without looking away from the computer, she explained, "You'll need to give me a few minutes, this could take some time to find them," and then looking over her glasses sternly reminded, "And we close at 5:00, you know."

"Yes ma'am, and thanks for your time!" I responded apologetically, then sat next to Dave and bounced both legs. Dave placed his hand on my shoulder.

"It's her job, you know," Dave offered.

"I know, thanks." I tossed him an affectionate wink.

After the clerk handed me the documents, I sat down to take in the somber information.

Christian "John" Dieterich's record named Christena as his mother. She must have been Gottlieb's first wife! Christena didn't figure much in the family lore because she died young and another took her place. Magdalena. I began to see a new piece of the puzzle coming into focus. Christena didn't get to watch her son grow. John would have been only 6-years-old when his mother died. But his life was proof of her life.

I recognized that John, robbed of his mother at a young age, would have had little comfort nor time to grieve. John likely learned to run the family farm, because as the oldest son, that was his birthright; his responsibility, age notwithstanding.

My finger moved down the page to the cause of death: Logging accident.

Farming was a seven-to-eight-month endeavor. The rest of the year, the livelihood of many a man and boy in northern Michigan was in harvesting pine, fir and spruce trees. And as soon as John was old enough — past puberty — he would have been accompanying Gottlieb on day and week-long logging trips, because mouths must be fed, no matter what time of year.

Emily Bingham writes of Michigan's lumber boom; it was an era defined by *the huge, the heroic, and the heartbreaking. The trees were massive, the work was dangerous and often deadly, the scale of it all — from the wealth amassed to the forests felled and forever changed — unlike anything the state had seen.*[3]

As the document before me stated, the Dieterich's knew firsthand logging's deadly dangers. John's service to his family would not be rewarded with a young wife to dote on his strength and industry, nor children with which to farm his own acreage. Rather, Gottlieb would have returned from that fateful trip alone with an unspeakable memory. Further, his role as father of a large family would have prevented him from taking time off to grieve. He would have informed the family of the loss, buried his son, and returned to logging, suffering in silence.

John Dieterich was killed by log timber on March 18, 1905, at the age of 18. John's line in our family was cut down too early, like his mother. Indeed, death

[3]Bingham, Emily. Century Old Photos Show the Epic Scale of Michigan's Lumber Era. MLive, July 15, 2018. https://www.mlive.com/news/2018/07/vintage_lumber_camp_photos.html

was a way of life for the Dieterich family.

Fifteen years after John's death, sister Harriet, daughter of Gottlieb and Magdalena, died at the age of 13, during the influenza pandemic, also known as Spanish flu, which had started in 1918 and continued into 1920.

Living in northern Michigan in a rural farming and logging region offered no safety from the reach of the flu. Emmet County, where the Dieterich's lived, was one of the counties hit hardest in all of Michigan. The 1918 pandemic infected nearly 500 million Americans, and took the lives of millions of people in four waves, between February 1918 to April 1920. Symptoms included skull-splitting headaches, high fevers with body aches, and bleeding from the nose, ears, and mouth.[4]

A mere two years after Harriet died, death visited the family once again, when Gottlieb suffered a stroke at the age of 64. His body must have been worn. Tired. It must've been a long, hard life as a farmer and logger in Northern Michigan.

I paused to gather my thoughts; then continued reading.

The tragedies continued. Three years after Gottlieb, Magdalena died of breast cancer, barely 50 years old. As Gottlieb's second wife, she had given birth to Matilda, Carl, Martha, Harriet, Emma and Amelia.

Death encompassed the Dieterich children. I remembered Martha.

We pulled up at the Petoskey city curb and knocked loudly on Aunt Martha's side door. She lived in an apartment in a large multi-unit home on Ingalls and Jefferson Streets, owned by Harriet, my 2nd cousin and Martha's niece. After rattling the lock, the door opened, delicious smells wafting our way. Aunt Martha greeted us with grandmotherly pats on the back, and we followed suit. She invited us to have a seat at the metal Sears & Roebuck kitchen table. Martha, once a sturdy caretaker of elderly clients, carefully carried the food from the stovetop, wearing a dainty yellow-checkered apron and a cotton summer dress. Her short gray-wiry hair was neatly held in place by a net decorated with tiny shimmering beads, a touch of old lady style.

She served us a hearty meal of mushroom meatballs, mashed potatoes, house slaw and pickled beets on Corningware — not the soup she had mentioned when I had called to arrange the visit. While it was special to be there, and the food tasty, the meal was uncomfortably quiet. It must have been hard for Aunt Martha to engage in conversation with such significant hearing loss. Dave and I did our best to make small talk: I complimented the food she had prepared, asked about her church, if she made the potholders she was using, and if she had any recipes I could copy. Martha answered with a few words, some smiles and nods, and not much more. But she beamed while serving us each a slice of homemade rhubarb pie with a scoop of vanilla ice cream. Martha was a good cook and knew it; but she humbly downplayed our praise.

After dinner, she invited us into the living room, adjacent to the galley kitchen, to enjoy a cup of Lipton tea. Dave and I settled into a floral couch dizzy with reds, oranges and greens. She proudly displayed handmade crocheted pillows, evidence of her resourcefulness. Aunt Martha sat across from us in a glider rocking chair, beside a basket of yarn and a Christian devotional book. I could no longer hold back; out poured the questions.

"Aunt Martha, Dave and I were in Brutus the other day and we came upon Christena Dieterich's gravestone. I did some digging at the courthouse, and I learned that she was Gottlieb's first wife; born in Germany. Do you know anything about their immigration?" I asked while pulling out a legal-pad from my backpack.

Immigration was something that lived in my family history, but the stories had been buried under years of sediment. It was curious, and bothered me a little. Dave's family had immigrated from Greece in the early 20th century and his grandparents and other family members openly shared stories of this period from the time he was old enough to comprehend them. Stories of his ancestors flowed out of him and appeared as an ornate tapestry rich with color. I was determined to create my own.

I was surprised when Aunt Martha opened like a flower bud, unfolding the story of her family, petal by petal. As she spoke, she wiped tears from her watery eyes with a small white handkerchief, "Oh yes. Christena Dieterich was my father's first wife. They came to America from Germany with a group of friends from the Evangelical Church in Murrhardt. This was in the late 1800s. They were running away to avoid service in the German military, and injured themselves in some way to escape the draft. When they arrived in North America, the group first landed in St. John's

Newfoundland. That's in Canada."

She paused to take a sip of tea. This was probably more talking than she had done in days. I told myself, *it's ok to sit for a minute, slow down and let Martha's pace lead you.* I took a sip of tea too.

She went on. "They lived in Ontario a few years before traveling across the border to Michigan. That's where my father married Christena." I listened intently, feverishly scribbling notes. Hearing the family history for the first-time lit firecrackers in my mind; but I was determined to keep myself in check... I didn't want to interrupt Aunt Martha's flow of memories, so I took a deep-breath and wiggled my toes to quell my excitement.

"John Klenk came to Brutus before the others. He came to scout out the area, and grew fond of it. The forests and hills reminded him of their hometown in Germany," she said.

I was eager to learn more about her family, so I interrupted: "Aunt Martha, after Christena died, how did Gottlieb meet your mother Magdalena?" I asked.

"My mother had been living with her parents in the old Mennonite settlement in Alanson. She was hired to help with the five children and farm work. We called them the first family. My father and she eventually got married and the second family began."

I felt as if I'd just taken a shot of whiskey. *Eventually got married? What? What did that mean? What did that look like? Romance? A love affair? An arrangement of convenience?* Dave and I exchanged a smile. This was getting interesting.

"In 1905, we moved a few miles away from the homestead to a two-story farmhouse on Brutus Road. The homestead was just a log cabin, and pretty crowded for our big family. So, we moved closer to my grandparents John and Harriet Kilmer, who had us over weekly for Sunday meals." At this memory, Aunt Martha seemed to get lost in her thoughts for a moment, until she nonchalantly offered, "Would you like to see a few photos and things I have stored away?"

Would I! Before I could say yes, Martha was up on her feet walking to her dimly lit bedroom. I flashed Dave a giddy expression over my shoulder as I got up to assist her. Dave followed close behind and turned on the lights. There in the corner of the room sat a well-worn steamer trunk wrapped in leather, bound with wood and locked with rusted metal clasps. Her cache. A time capsule. A treasure trove with artifacts locked away for years. Martha twiddled with opening this well-travelled trunk that had been hauled over the decades on carriages, trains, and even in her own car. It looked weathered but sturdy. Like her. As she opened the lid, the air filled with a musty scent, like an antique store. I sneezed into the crook of my right arm, my left holding Aunt Martha's elbow.

"Are you feeling alright, dear?" Martha asked.

Touched by her tenderness, I replied. "Oh yes, Aunt Martha! I'm feeling fine. It's just allergies."

Martha asked for a chair, so she could sit and look through the items in the trunk. Dave hurried into the kitchen to grab one, and I knelt beside Martha as she unhurriedly pulled out a collection of photographs in plastic sheaths, newspaper clippings, books, and postcards and placed them on the bed. After a few minutes, Dave suggested he carry the items back to the living room where he gently placed the artifacts on the coffee table. Martha collapsed back into her rocker blowing out a sigh, and again wiped her eyes to look more closely at a faded sepia photograph I was holding up with care. It looked at least 100 years old.

"My father homesteaded the land together with the German immigrants, and built a log cabin on Red School Road, in Brutus where I was born. See him, there on top of the logs? They were used to build our home!" Martha said in her shaky voice, now a little more vital than earlier.

The photograph was unlike any I had ever seen: a group of men, all clad in shirtsleeves, suspenders, and farm boots, displaying felled logs like trophies.

I picked up another weathered piece of paper and held it up. "Is this newspaper clipping about the Germans who came to Brutus?"

"Oh yes. Yes. Some of the names were spelled wrong, but those are settlers who homesteaded on Red School Road."

"Aunt Martha," I said louder than I needed to, "do you have a photograph of the log home you were born in?" I was dying to see what it looked like. I flashed back to a precious memory of a time when Dad helped me build a miniature log cabin for a school project.

Martha interrupted my memory, "No, no. No picture of the cabin. And

OLD SETTLERS IN MAPLE River township are shown in this picture taken about 70 years ago. In the group are: Mr. and Mrs. Charles Kugler, Mr. and Mrs. Jacob Shrier (Schreier), Charlie Kuebler, Mr. and Mrs. John Klink (Klenk), Mr. and Mrs. John Wurst, Mr. and Mrs. Gottlieb Dieterich and a brother to Mr. Shrier (Schreier). The picture was brought in by Mrs. Frieda Buchhorn of Petoskey.

Thursday, June 15, 1950, Northern Michigan Review

I was only four years old when we moved to the farm house, so I don't remember much."

I tried to conceal my disappointment and moved on, pulling Gottlieb's obituary from the stack of memorabilia.

Listed on the obit were the names of the surviving 9 children and the dates of Gottlieb's arrival to Ontario, Canada, in August of 1881.

At the time of Gottlieb's death, he had lived in America for 39 years. What a remarkable accomplishment: to have said goodbye to his parents and siblings in Wurttemberg never to see them again; to have traveled under duress with little income; to have moved from Canada to America and homesteaded the land; to have raised eleven children and lived to the age of 64 as a subsistence farmer.

I turned my attention back to Martha, wondering how she fared as a young adult seeking financial stability of her own, "Aunt Martha, how old were you when you moved away from the farm?"

"When I was only 16, I moved from the farm to live and work as a housekeeper in Petoskey."

"Wait, 16? You're kidding! At 16 I was still arguing with my parents about making my bed and doing the dishes, and you had to move away from home to support yourself?" I was stunned. Martha nodded with a proud smile and silent chuckle.

"It's just how it was back then. We had to grow up sooner than kids do today. In fact, I didn't know how to cook very well because my older sister Matilda did most of the cooking with Mom on the farm, so I had to learn from the other housekeepers." She paused, thinking. "I earned $6.00 per week," she laughed. I worked there until the owner died. The family gave me a beautiful oil painting and some linens when I left."

Then Martha's mood changed, as she glimpsed a photograph of her sister Harriet. Martha quietly shared about Harriet falling ill during the influenza pandemic and how she moved back to Brutus for a time to help the family as they struggled to care for Harriet while also dealing with the daily responsibilities of the farm. Martha appeared pensive, "She had beautiful red hair. Unfortunately, she didn't survive."

Sweeping her emotions under cover, Martha adjusted her body in the chair and continued. "Back in Petoskey for my second job, I worked for the Curtis

GOTTLEIB DIETRICH, PIONEER RESIDENT OF BRUTUS, DIES WEDNESDAY.

Brutus and the surrounding community were shocked Wednesday afternoon by the unexpected death of Christian Gottleib Dietrich, one of the pioneer farmers of the Brutus country. Mr. Dietrich had been in his usual good health and following his mid-day meal had just left the house when he was seized by a heart attack.

Mr. Dietrich was born in Wurttenberg, Germany, August 29, 1856. He came on Ontario, in August, 1881, and from there to Brutus in November, 1883. Since then he has resided at Brutus.

Surviving him are the widow and nine children: Mrs. Paul Brower, of North Bay, Charlevoix county; Mrs. Jesse McDowell, of Petoskey; Miss Bertha Dietrich, of New York; Mrs. Frank Palmer, of Epsilon; Carl Dietrich, of Brutus; Mrs. Frank Schmidt, of Kegomic; Miss Martha Dietrich, of Petoskey, and Miss Emma and Miss Amelia Dietrich, of Brutus.

Funeral from the German Evangelical church of Brutus Saturday afternoon at 2 o'clock. Rev. F. W. Krueger, of Petoskey, in charge. Burial at Brutus.

April 13, 1922, Petoskey Evening News

41

family as a maid: I made beds, dusted, cleaned dishes and waited tables. They were a wealthy family; Mr. Curtis was the head of a national bank in downtown Petoskey. They had two boys a couple years younger than I was."

"Aunt Martha", I offered, "I also worked as a maid while attending college, cleaning houses for wealthy clients, and at the same time as a waitress at a local family diner in order to make ends meet." She smiled with a knowing expression. An approving expression. I felt connected to her in a new way. Not merely as relatives, but as sisters.

Martha closed her eyes for a moment to rest, and I paused to observe this strong, diligent, humble woman before me. Great-Aunt Martha. Knee-high stockings covering varicose veins, bare knobby knees showing slightly under the hem of her skirt, sagging breasts and wrinkled pink lips. A portal to the past. A foundation for my present. This was my living ancestor. Awakened to this perspective, I felt profound gratitude. Peace. I had found my people.

With empathy I slowly proceeded, "So what happened with your family after your parents passed away?"

Without skipping a beat, she opened her eyes and began speaking again, tired but resolute, "I left my job at the Curtis house to move home when my mother was ill, and to help Carl and the girls; Emma was 14 and Amelia 11." Aunt Martha appeared distant and stoic while describing the family trauma. Rather than give emotional details, she spoke of the ways she supported the family financially.

"While I lived back on the farm, I worked as the postmaster in Brutus for a summer, earning my pay per cancelled stamp, in addition to working on the farm, and selling butter, pickles and eggs at local markets. I also worked for Nellie Purple at the Purple Inn in Brutus as a waitress. They were known for having family-style chicken dinners. One time Eleanor Roosevelt visited because her daughter Anna went to a prestigious girl's camp on Burt Lake at Indian Point." She paused and smiled. "I had the unique privilege of waiting on her at the Purple Inn. Mrs. Purple's chicken dinners were famous."

I looked over at Dave with shock. He shrugged his shoulders and said, "Aunt Martha that is amazing! Do you know the name of the camp where Anna attended?"

"I believe it was called Pinewood," she answered. I resolved to find out more about this unbelievable detail!

Next, I pulled out a yellowed report card from the now scattered documents covering the small table. It was one of Martha's from the small Brutus school she attended as a child. "I see here you received good grades!" Seizing on the opportunity to explore another topic, I asked, "What was school like growing up?"

"School? Well, my brother Carl was superintendent of the school in Brutus for a time. He would go every morning to make sure school started promptly. I graduated from eighth grade. These days they push most students to graduate from college, but I wonder who will do all the general labor if everyone has a college degree?"

I became uncomfortable and self-conscious. *I was a college graduate.* Martha and her siblings had been workers — physical laborers — and proud of it. They were strong and resourceful. They had survived on their own terms. I knew little of the life they had lived. I changed the subject, "Tell me about your church."

"Oh, well we attended the German Evangelical Church in Brutus. At first, when the Germans settled, they had church in people's homes until they could construct the church building on Red School Road. Carl, Matilda, Emma and I were all baptized and confirmed in that church."

"How did you get to church from the farm? That must have been more than 3 miles?"

Martha grinned at my interest. "We rode to church on a wagon carriage. Pulled by horses. Others laughed at us because it wasn't like theirs. In the winter they put the wagon box on sleighs and put some straw inside for the ride. Sometimes they warmed bricks to keep our feet warm. One time I received a very special tea cup and tea pot from a friend in my Sunday School class for Christmas," she paused and looked out the window.

I waited to allow Aunt Martha to rest a minute. This must have been more talking and remembering than she had done in a long, long while. But rather than stopping, she seemed to rally with increased energy. "Do you have any other questions?"

Not one to let the opportunity pass me by, I jumped back into the conversation. "Can you tell me about your life on the farm?"

I noticed Martha start to rock the rocking chair back and forth as she gathered her thoughts. She pointed to a photograph on the corner of the table of someone on a tractor. "Well, you know, life on the farm was, I guess, normal. Lots of families had farms. It's how we all survived." She kept rocking, and fiddled with a blanket covering her lap. "We ate what we grew, or raised, or picked: potatoes, corn, garden vegetables, fruit, pickles, cows, chickens, pigs. Our orchard was filled with apple trees, pear trees, and cherry and crabapple trees. My father Gottlieb played music with a pear leaf, and he enjoyed playing the accordion. He was always telling jokes, but had a habit of drinking too much home-brewed apple cider."

I reflected on the hundred-year-old apple tree at the site of the former log cabin. Secrets revealed. I remembered Dad saying that Grandma Emma disdained alcohol, and even had prayed that my dad wouldn't take up drinking. Then I remembered counting the empty beer cans when Dad had a bad day at work. Anxiety surfaced; my cheeks felt hot. I changed the subject again.

"Did you have any regular chores Aunt Martha?"

"Yes. Yes. It was a little different for me. Since my parents only had one son, after John died, Matilda worked inside to help Mom, so I helped with the boys' work outside. I helped take care of the cows and crops. I drove the horse pulley to lift hay into the barn. Hard work. It was all hard work. We had two horses, one named Maude and another Jim, a western horse we broke in." Martha got a big grin on her face. "One time Carl was loading hay onto the wagon, while Emma and Amelia were stomping it down. The horses got spooked and took off running, knocking the girls to their seats, screaming for help. Thankfully, the reins got snagged on a gate and the girls were ok. That Jim was one wild horse!"

"That must have been so scary! I rode a horse once at a church youth group function that took off so fast, I thought I'd die!"

Dave chimed in, "Martha, did you have any modern conveniences on the farm?"

"Not until Carl and I were running the farm. We got a hay loader, tractor, refrigerator, and a washing machine! That was a big deal back then," she laughed.

A memory appeared in my mind. "Martha, as a little girl I picked berries with our friends the Blanks on their property in Harbor Springs. Did you pick berries?"

"Yes, in the spring and summer, we picked wild huckleberries at Carp Lake and wild raspberries, red and black ones, in the hills. We canned them for winter, along with apple butter."

I responded, "Your family must have looked forward to berry season! I get all my berries at the grocery store year-round."

"Times certainly have changed!" she chuckled. "But we did go to the store, too. We went to the general store in Brutus to sell things or receive credit for potatoes, pickles, eggs and butter. Most household supplies were either bought in Brutus or Pellston. Our clothing was mostly handmade; my mother bought material and shoes in Pellston. Occasionally, the Watkins man would come to visit, selling a variety of goods like kitchen spices. And the Indians would sell their baskets door to door."

"Wait, there were Indians that lived nearby?" I was surprised.

"Oh my, yes. Yes, there were Indians that lived very nearby. Once I went to a pow-wow in Cross Village. And one of my sisters, Louise Brower, who lived on Bay Shore Road with her husband Paul, adopted an American Indian girl who had been living in an orphanage." She paused, and I thought she was finished; but she then spoke up, saying, "And I heard something about a *Burn-Out* that occurred before I was born."

I was intrigued and had no knowledge of where Indians might have lived or even still lived in Michigan. Indians were a group of people I learned about from involvement in a YMCA Indian Maidens Troupe. I had hoped to press Aunt Martha for more details to learn more, but we'd already been there nearly three hours, and Aunt Martha's eyes looked weary and her voice had begun to falter; it was clearly time to go. Dave and I poured out words of gratitude for the meal and memories. Martha patted me on the shoulder as I hugged her feeble frame. She invited us to come again.

I waved good-bye and said, "Thank you, Aunt Martha, for your stories! They are like precious gems."

Aunt Martha laughed nervously, embarrassed by the attention. Her eyes told us differently. We pulled away from the curb and let it all soak in.

exploring the homestead

I was possessed. I couldn't sleep, so I got out of bed at 4:00 AM to re-read my notes. At breakfast I apologized to Dave for this interruption to our easy-going nonchalant schedule, kissed his forehead goodbye, and left the cottage to head back to Petoskey. At the courthouse once again, I clicked down the hall in heels, but stopped in my tracks at the glass doors, taken aback by my reflection. I noticed similarities in my face with Aunt Martha. I smiled.

I was back to uncover more details on the Dieterich family's history. In particular — at this point — I wanted to know exactly when Gottlieb remarried after his first wife's death. I complimented Sharon, the clerk, on her smart outfit. She recognized me this time, and greeted me with a smile.

"Today I'm in need of a marriage record!" I said confidently.

"Are you a genealogist?" she asked.

"Well..." I hadn't thought of myself as a genealogist, but perhaps she was right. "Yes, actually!"

"Interesting. Give me a few minutes to finish what I'm working on and I'll find the document."

Interesting indeed! I thought of myself as a teacher and a wannabe writer, but never a genealogist. With that, Sharon returned and placed the record on the counter, as I fished the cash out of my purse to pay the requisite fee. She wrote up a receipt and pushed both the receipt and the document across the counter to me with a smile, then returned to her desk.

Christena died in February of 1892. According to the marriage record, Gottlieb married Magdalena in June of 1892, only four months later. Four months! Clearly this marriage was a necessity. There were five young children, a log home, and a 40-acre farm to care for. At the time of Christena's death, the first family, as Martha called it, consisted of four girls and one boy: Louisa- age 11, Mollie- age 9, Bertha- age 8 and Christine and John, twins age 6.

I wondered how Dave and I would cope if similar circumstances befell us. It was difficult to imagine. I didn't want to entertain the thought that Dave or I would lose each other at such a young age. I certainly couldn't fathom marrying someone I hadn't had time to get to know and fall in love with. But those modern luxuries of relationships were not readily available to Gottlieb as a 34-year-old widower with five children, nor to the unmarried 18-year-old woman with no viable marriage prospects. Nonetheless, at some point between February and June of 1892 Gottlieb would have met privately with Magdalena's parents, John and Harriet Kilmer, and made his offer of marriage.

My mind swirled with myriad curiosities. I couldn't imagine how Magdalena felt about the prospect of marriage to a man nearly twice her age. Was she scared or resistant? Did she beg her parents to let her stay in the comfort of their home? Did she have a choice? Did he treat her well? Did she ever really love him?

An anxious fear surfaced from the past, catching me by surprise. Memories when my "NO!" wasn't honored. When my voice was silenced by the forceful voice of another. Memories when the voice of a man belittled my dignity, raising his voice and lowering my self-regard. *Breathe. Remember what your therapist taught you. What is true? What's the evidence for the message you're internalizing?*

I hadn't banked on this part of being a genealogist. Learning about others in the past is one thing; reckoning with my own was quite another. I walked back over to Sharon, to re-focus my attention. "Hi, I'm so sorry to bother you, but can I do a little more work in the records room?" I asked. She must have recognized my tears and responded sweetly this time.

"Sure, no problem."

Now that I knew the date of the remarriage, I needed to find the home that Gottlieb and Magdalena would later make together. Where the first family and second family would form and fledge. I needed to find the address for the farmhouse.

Sharon showed me where to look. "You can find the deed and description in this area. Good luck!" She turned without saying anything else, and left me alone, which was nice.

Soon, I found a record for each of the Dieterich's homes, and their locations. For the first property on Red School Road, Gottlieb paid $400.00 for 40 acres in 1884. This seemed inexpensive, but at that time in history, a wagon cost $65.00 and a horse $200.00. The land required the hard work of felling trees, severing roots, leveling the ground for planting, and more. For the second property, the two-story home and 40 acres on Brutus Road, he paid $624.00 in 1902. The new property moved them away from the German settlement on Red School Road. They would be farther away from their friends and community, the children, all eight of them, would have to attend a different school. Yet they were closer to Magdalena's parents who resided in Alanson.

With the address scratched on a paper in my pocket, it was time to visit the family farm, but Dave would want to join me. So, I returned to Indian River to pick him up for our next adventure. I showed up in my usual fashion and declared, "You've got to come with me! I've got the address of the farmhouse!" Dave wasn't even in the house. He was on the deck, reading a book. I walked through the kitchen, opened the screen and made my declaration once again: "I've got the address to the farmhouse! Get in the car; we're going to find it!" I headed to the bedroom to change.

Dave chuckled (and maybe rolled his eyes) and followed me into the bedroom to pull on a t-shirt and slide on his Birkenstocks. "You're hilarious, Jules. Like a little girl..." I interrupted Dave with a hug and whispered in his ear, "I know, I know. It's just all so amazing. Oh, Dave...thank you for being my partner in this!" We got into the car and sped off.

———————

Before going to the farmhouse, I wanted to take a quick detour to find the graves of Magdalena's parents — my great-great-grandparents, Harriet and John Kilmer. So we headed to the Mennonite Church where I had first discovered Christena's gravestone. No longer reluctant to pull up on the church lawn, Dave decisively parked the car, and we both got out of the car quickly. We found the gravestones within seconds. I noticed that Harriet's maiden name — Snyder — was engraved into her tombstone, along with her married name; an uncommon practice at the time. I thought this indicative of a strong woman with a prominent family name. A declaration in stone that this was a woman of importance. Harriet lived a long life of 86 years, outlasting her husband by 11. She had been supportive of her daughter Magdalena and grandchildren. By having weekly family meals, she kept a watchful eye on them. The grave of John, my great-great-grandfather, was next to her, as were several of their sons. I knelt to touch the stones and wished I too could have been invited to a family meal. Inexplicably, I felt love for these ancestors I could never meet.

We left the church and headed east on Brutus Road looking for a farmhouse with the numbers 7896. Dave drove us past a handful of homes, some ranches, a two-story farmhouse with wrap around front porch, and then one that appeared completely abandoned with broken-out windows, near an old wooden barn.

"I think we just passed it!" I blurted out, feeling overjoyed, yet apprehensive about trespassing on the abandoned property. Dave downshifted and made a quick U-turn at Snyder Road — Snyder... a name I recognized — then turned onto the barely visible driveway we had just passed. The house and barns were surrounded by a jungle of overgrown plants and trees; as Dave pulled in, the high grass on the driveway brushed up against the car's undercarriage, and sticks crunched beneath the tires.

I opened the door before the car was in park. Dave chastised, "Julie, hold on a minute!"

But I was undeterred. Stepping out of the car, I took a few steps and scanned the property. No longer an operating farm, fields where crops once grew were full of weeds. The massive wood barn with a rusty red roof, sat securely upon a foundation of multi-colored and massive stones. There were pines surrounding the acreage as a border, and in the distance, hills and forest met the sky. Turning toward the house, I leapt over a sea of grasses and made my way to the back stoop. The two-story, dilapidated, wood-sided house badly needed a coat of paint, but still looked inhabitable. I stepped on to the concrete pad outside the door, and checked the back door. I turned the rickety knob. It opened. This would be risky, but I was here, and I wasn't going to miss this opportunity. I announced to Dave, who was checking out the chicken coop, "I'm going in!"

Dave said, "Jules! Wait for me!"

Easing the door open, I cast my gaze around what I could see of the house. We stepped in, but gingerly. Each step required careful calculation to test the floor boards, making sure they were stable before transferring our weight. "Julie, are you sure we should be snooping around in here?" Dave asked. He was always the voice of reason, but this was not a time for logic. It was a time for adventure.

"No, I'm not sure! But I'm gonna do it anyway! You can stay outside if you want... I've got to explore this place, Dave!"

I kept on. Broken glass and remnants of garbage carelessly strewn about littered the floor from the last owner, and maybe some other trespassers (I mean, adventurers) like us. Great-Uncle Carl and Aunt Martha would not have approved of this mess. Through the small mud room we entered another door into a square kitchen with three windows overlooking a mature pine tree and the barn. The front door opened to a porch with a collapsed roof. I recalled a photo of Martha's, in which the family posed while sitting on the porch with straight faces. No frivolous smiles for them.

Maneuvering past a sleeping potbelly stove whose brick foundation was crumbling at the corners, we entered a well-lit north-facing rectangular living room with a low ceiling, a 15' x 20' space. Tree limbs scratched at a window where curtains flailed through broken glass, like spirits dancing. "Creepy!" Out the side windows a row of apple trees looked barren and forgotten.

At the back of the room, we continued through a door into a small bedroom, likely Gottlieb and Magdalena's, just big enough for a bed and a dresser, no closet. Through the rear window I could see the outhouse. "Can you imagine having to go to the bathroom in the middle of a winter night?" I asked.

Dave ripped a pun. "That would have been really crappy!" I rolled my eyes.

Around the corner, a stairway led to the second floor. I glanced inquisitively at Dave who shrugged his shoulders and said, "You can go. I'm not."

The wood creaked under my feet as I ascended the stairs. At the top, I looked right, then left, where two bedrooms would have housed the eight children, one for two boys and one for six girls. I imagined the sisters snuggled tightly together on a hay-stuffed mattress under a handmade quilt, and wondered: *Did they laugh like my sister and I, playing games in the dark when they were supposed to be sleeping? Did they complain about bossy friends or admit to having crushes on boys? Did they talk about having their period for the first time? Six girls. That's a lot of PMS!* I snickered.

"What's so funny?" Dave asked standing at the bottom of the stairway.

"Oh nothing..." I slowly descended the stairs, returning to the main floor.

Through a small door next to the kitchen, we found the pantry where canned food and root vegetables would have been stored, and a passage to an eerie basement that even I dared not enter. I wanted to find a keepsake from the past, but no such luck. What I did find, however, was something to root my imagination. A place where my people had actually lived. I had visions of the family gathering for a meal, of the sibling's doing homework, of Magdalena sewing dresses, of Gottlieb puffing on a pipe.

Site of Dieterich property on Brutus Road, Brutus, Michigan

Photos by Nate Pappas

We departed the house as we had entered, and traipsed around back to look in the outhouse and chicken coop. I investigated each one sensibly, but still driven by the spirit of adventure and the "if not now, then when?" attitude that possessed me. When I got over to the massive rough-hewn barn, I tried to open the large sliding barn door, but rust, bent metal, and warped wood supports made that impossible. So, I did the next reasonable thing and snuck through an opening where a plank was missing. Climbing up the stone foundation a couple of feet, I had to push myself up enough to get a knee into the opening so I could crawl through. I was a little girl again, exploring on the campground — but this time imagination and reality were merging. As I rose to my feet in the barn, a loose plank of wood scratched my back.

"Ouch!" I piped.

"Are you OK? Julie this is dangerous!"

"Come on Dave! This is so cool!" I said convincingly, rubbing the pain away.

The afternoon sun shone through dozens of cracks in the walls creating a holy mist of light. On the main level, a rusty-skeletal combine appeared as a giant, metal dinosaur, taking up a third of the floor space. I tip-toed over toward a ladder to avoid stepping in guano. Looking up at the hay loft, I was taken aback to memories of jumping onto hay bales from high places and sliding down chutes at a family friend's farm. I climbed the ladder to examine how the conveyor system would have carried hay bales up for storage, but I was smart enough not jump this time.

A creaky door nearly fell of the hinges as we opened it, leading to a lower level. We made our way down the stone and earthen steps and looked around. We surmised it was the area where the family milked the cows. Troughs lined the walls where the "bastards" — as my uncle Carl called them — would have eaten side by side. Stone walls held up the barn floor above our heads. A dirt floor thick with hay and manure worked its way into the crevices of our shoes.

"Good thing I changed out of those heels!" I laughed.

"Good thing I came with you!" Dave replied.

In one corner, lit by a window with broken glass, I found a dusty old medicine bottle, and a rusted-out license plate. "Artifacts! I'm taking them." I cheered.

We escaped out the back door where cows would have entered and exited at milking time, to an overgrown field where asparagus once flourished. The sight was serene, breathtaking. I voiced, "I wonder if the family ever got a break from their labor to enjoy the beauty of this place. It's like a landscape painting by Monet." Hearing this gave Dave an idea, and for Christmas that year, he gifted me with a painting of the barn and fields.

As we walked wistfully back to the car, grasshoppers catapulted like popcorn with each step. We were startled by a family of wild turkeys scurrying out of our way to take cover under the long arms of a white pine.

I said goodbye to the house and the barn, to the spirits of my deceased ancestors. An Amish family wearing black bonnets trotted past on a horse-pulled wagon.

"Julie," Dave whispered, "Can you believe it!" He squeezed my hand before backing out.

We drove back to the main road and found the newer Mennonite church, located in town in the old schoolhouse building. There were cars in the parking lot, and emboldened by this spirit of adventure, I decided to see who was inside. Dave parked the car, and reluctantly-but-supportively accompanied me into the narthex of the church where a group of ladies were quilting. They looked like my great-aunts. I felt a desire to sit down and start sewing, but rather asked for their pardon, and told them who I was and what I was up to. They generously suggested I talk to a local historian named Wilson Snider. I wondered if perhaps he was related to my great-great-grandmother Harriet Snyder Kilmer. One of the women said the Sniders lived just down the street, and were, more than likely, home.

I thanked the women and turned to exit the building. As we walked energetically to the car, Dave looked at me as if I was off my rocker and said, "We're going to the Snider's house, aren't we?"

"Are you kidding me? Of course we are!" I replied." If you don't mind, of course."

Dave laughed and said, "Why not, we're already in this knee-deep!" He knew me well-enough to know that I was on a mission and I would take it wherever it led.

The Sniders lived near the old Mennonite church, in a two-story house with tar-paper siding. As we stepped out of the car, someone peeked through the curtains. People didn't receive many unannounced visitors in these parts. I knocked at the front door, tucked my hands in my pockets, and smiled with a non-threatening expression, or so I hoped. A cat meowed and sauntered by; his tail slapped my calf as if to say, "Be gone stranger!" He scampered away, hiding behind some hollyhocks as Wilson Snider opened the door with his good hand; the other was missing.

"Hello, may I help you?" he asked skeptically.

"I'm so sorry to bother you. I am a relative of Martha and Emma Dieterich who grew up in Brutus. Some ladies at the Mennonite church in town suggested I stop by, saying that you are a local historian," I voiced in one quick breath.

He responded, "Oh, ah, wait here." He disappeared while I nervously picked at hang nails. A few minutes later, he returned with his wife.

"Come in. We have a minute to spare," he said with a twinkle in his eye. Small town hospitality. His wife was drying her hands on an apron. They pointed to a sofa and invited us to have a seat. "My name is Wilson Snider. My wife here is Barbara."

"It's so nice to meet you! Thank you for talking with us. I'm Julie and this is my husband David. I have been doing some research on my family history and wondered if you had any information about the Dieterich and Kilmer families," I said as I was getting positioned on the sofa.

Barbara answered, "Oh my. Well, Wilson here loves to talk about history!" Wilson took a seat across from us on a Laz-E-Boy chair, and Barbara went to the kitchen to bring us some water and a plate of store-bought Windmill cookies. She set them on the coffee table next to a magazine.

Dave and I sat close together on the plaid sofa, occasionally tossing each other reassuring smiles. Barbara joined Wilson in another comfortable chair; sitting next to each other, they looked alike with gray hair, withered warm faces and rosy cheeks. As I described the search I'd been on, they listened intently. Then Wilson excused himself to fetch a large binder, and returned with a genealogy he had written about the Snider family.

"So if Martha is your great-aunt, then we are cousins! Martha and I are second cousins because her grandmother, Harriet Snyder Kilmer, was my great-aunt! I've been working on this history for years and have followed the Snider family back to the birth of my ninth great-grandfather Hans Jacob Schneider born in Bern, Switzerland, 1536 (or 1534)." Wilson took a deep breath. "Hans moved to Germany during the Reformation movement, as a non-conformist, and subscribed to the teachings of Menno Simmons. My fourth great-grandfather, Jacob Snider or Snyder, came to America from Germany and lived in Lancaster, Pennsylvania, where he met and married his wife, Maria Hershey — yes, part of THE Hershey family — and your great-great-grandmother Harriet moved to Brutus from the Elkhart area in northern Indiana, but she was born in Waterloo, Ontario." He paused and smiled a big, satisfied smile.

"Wow! This is amazing! I am in awe of your research Mr. Snider. You are the real deal! I knew I was German, but Swiss too!" I took a moment to consider the implications of what Wilson just said. I continued, "So, I think this means that Hans Jacob Schneider is my 11th great-grandfather. This is hard to fathom!" I was already planning a trip to the Swiss Alps and thinking about buying a Swiss cookbook! "Have you ever traveled to Switzerland?" I naively asked.

"No, but I did serve in the U.S. Peace Corps during WWII. If you were wondering how this happened (he held up his stub), I'd like to say I lost it in the war, but actually it was due to an accident at a tannery where I worked when I was 26. I received $3500 in the settlement which we used to purchase 200 acres. Some would've given an arm and a leg for that, but I only had to give an arm!" He chuckled.

"I'm sorry. How awful for you." I didn't know what more to say, but Wilson responded, perhaps sensing my discomfort and embarrassment.

"It's ok. That was over 40 years ago. I've gotten along quite well with the help of my bride, Barbara." She acknowledged his compliment with a pat on the hand.

"Recently, I was at the Mennonite cemetery and found a Dieterich family member. Might you know why Christena Dieterich, Gottlieb's first wife, is buried there?" I asked.

"Sure, the cemetery she was buried in used to be the county cemetery." Wilson replied.

I responded with a nervous chuckle, "Well that makes sense! Do you know anything about the marriage of Gottlieb, who had been a member of the German Evangelical church, to Magdalena Kilmer, a member of the Mennonite church?"

Wilson sat up in his chair with a cheeky grin. "Actually, there is an old wives'

Mennonite Cemetery, Brutus
Photos by Nate Pappas

Wilson and Barbara Snider
Photo by Julie Dieterich Pappas

Brutus Post Office *Photo by Laura Isaacs*

tale, that Gottlieb hypnotized Magdalena so she would marry him....but truth be told, there may have been some opposition when they got married."

Secrets revealed. *Were they reproved by their communities? Had they become outsiders? Is this why people laughed as they trotted by with horse and carriage?* I was lost in my thoughts for a moment.

Dave, not wanting to wear out our welcome, made the move to say goodbye. We thanked Wilson and Barbara for opening their home to us and asked them to pose for a photo in the front yard. As we headed back to town, we saw them waving in the rear-view mirror.

"Well, that was amazing!" I began.

"I can't believe how much you have learned about your family in such a short amount of time! It's incredible. Let's celebrate and go out for dinner at Hoppies!"

"Really! I'd love that!"

At the crossroads, I noticed an "Open" sign at the Brutus Post Office. "Um, Dave, can we make one last stop before dinner? Please? Real quick! I just want to see where Aunt Martha worked!"

Dave waited in the car while I ventured inside. On the wall above a window, a display of black and white photos of bygone Brutus were hung in crude frames. There was one with the Purple Inn next to the train tracks and depot, another with L.E. Wagley & Co. General Merchandise, and a third was a landscape of Brutus showing the school house, homes, and a glimpse of main street on a winter's day. I wondered what happened to old Brutus. Champing at the bit, I boldly asked the postmaster, "Might I be able to borrow these photos in order to make replicas with a professional photographer?"

He looked at me as if I was crazy and said nothing. I continued, "I'll leave my driver's license here as a guarantee that I'll be sure to return them." I proceeded to tell him about my research and asked if he had a copy of the Yellow Pages. I looked up a reputable photographer in the Harbor Springs area and scribbled the number down on an envelope. I went out to the car and told Dave, "Take me across the street to the payphone." Dave looked at me quizzically. "Don't ask. Just go." He backed up and then drove across the street to a payphone at the gas station. I called the photographer in Harbor Springs to inquire about the possibility. He assured me they would take utmost care of the photos. Returning with this information, to my surprise, the postmaster agreed to my odd proposition! I handed him my driver's license and he took photos off the wall. "I'll be back!" I assured.

Photos of Brutus 1912 -13 William Howard Diebert

in the library

The next morning, I needed to drop off the Brutus Post Office photos with the professional photographer, Bruce G. Gathman, who showed me his archive-safe reproduction technique. I then made my way to the Petoskey Carnegie Library, to flesh out my knowledge about the area and times during which my relatives had lived. The building, an architectural beauty built in 1908 in the neoclassical revival style, received a *National Register of Historic Places* status. It was built with stone and brick, with a black ash interior.[5] The smell of old wood and old books confronted me as I entered the colossal front doors. I admired the ornate fireplace where I found an empty red-velvet chair to sit and make a plan.

First, I endeavored to figure out what happened to the town of Brutus that originated as a stagecoach stop on the mail route from Petoskey to Cheboygan. It's current state no longer resembled the Brutus in the photos I'd borrowed from the Post Office or seen at my Aunt Martha's. The librarian helped me locate a directory from 1911-12 where I discovered the town had once offered a complete collection of village proprietors: a general store, lumber mills, dressmaker, blacksmith, barber, hotel and restaurant, livery and boarding house, and four churches. Just the basics, but just enough for a farm community. I moved to the microfilm room to research newspapers that could shed light on the town's demise. I found an article that described its ghastly fate.

Petoskey Evening News: April 28, 1915

"For nearly five hours Wednesday morning it appeared as though the whole village would be destroyed by fire. Two store buildings, four residences, a blacksmith shop and two barns are the toll taken by the flames in the early morning fire. The fire was discovered shortly after 12 o'clock Wednesday morning in an old store building adjoining the building owned and occupied by Mr. Maxfield with his general store. The building had been used as a sort of club room by the ladies, who held socials and various meetings there. Tuesday evening a tramp was noticed hanging about the building and it is thought he might have set it on fire, or the fire he made to cook his meal might have been responsible for the damage."[6]

---

[5]Fought, Jeanne. Early Carnegie History. https://www.petoskeylibrary.org/en/about-the-library/history-of-the-library.aspx

[6]Petoskey Evening News, April 28, 1915, page 3.

Despite the devastation, the Dieterich family stayed in Brutus for many years. Still intact, they had a church, a school, a farm and a carriage on which they could travel to Pellston for supplies. I jotted down some reflections. *The Dieterich Family lived a simple life, not focused on materialism but rather idealism. They didn't have a mall to gape at the latest clothing trends like I do, or subscriptions to magazines in which I find new ideas for decorating my home every month. They didn't go to restaurants every weekend or have vacations every summer. They didn't even get a day off work for Christmas!*

I wondered how and why the Germans immigrated to America in the first place. As I examined documents, I learned they likely traversed the Atlantic by passenger liner, and then to Brutus via the railroads that had just been extended in 1882 to Mackinaw City. The trip from Germany would have taken about 8 days according to *The Geography of Transport Systems.*

> *By the 1860's, the introduction of iron hulls, compound steam engines, and screw propulsion significantly reduced crossing times to about 8-9 days. No longer limited by the technical limits of wood armatures, the size of liners increased substantially, with a tonnage exceeding 5,000 tons and a capacity of 1,500 passengers.*[7]

During this time in history, many Germans were coming to Michigan because Emigration agents had been sent to Germany to advertise the possibilities of homesteading land in publications and pamphlets. Americans viewed Germans as industrious and skilled, with the potential for cheap labor to advance the economy. In Germany, land was hard to come by due to inheritance laws, and couples often had to forgo marriage because of laws regarding financial constraints. As a result, many farming families experienced downward mobility, with little hope for future gains.

America offered a solution. Gottlieb could finally marry Christena once they had moved to Canada. Along with their German friends, they likely left without the government's permission. They would have secretly traveled at

---

[7]Paul-Rodrigue, Jean. The Geography of Transport Systems 6th Edition. Routledge, 2024.
https://transportgeography.org/contents/chapter1/emergence-of-mechanized-transportation-systems/liner-transatlantic-crossing-time/

night to the port for departure.[8] I was inspired by their spirit of adventure — by necessity — and found a sense of connection to them as a result.

Once the immigrants arrived in Brutus, they purchased land to homestead. $400, in Gottlieb's case. Land to clear. A log home to build to start and raise a family. Martha had been born in that log cabin built by her father. I recalled the photo of Gottlieb standing on top of an enormous stack of logs. The arduous process of clearing the land in order to grow crops was explained by Barbara Greenwood in *A Pioneer Sampler.*

First the area was under-brushed—all the bushes and small trees were cut down and piled for burning. After the trees had been felled, they were chopped or sawed into ten-foot lengths to make them easier to move. Some were dragged away by oxen to be used for building or fence-making. The rest were burned with the brushwood. On average, a settler could clear twenty-two acres in the first three years. The work was so hard the neighbors often held "bees" and worked together to help one another clear the land...Once cleared of trees, the field was still full of roots and covered with stumps. The roots could be grubbed out with a mattock (a kind of ax), but the stumps were so difficult to remove, that the first crops were planted around them.[9]

Knowing this dashed any romantic notions of wanting to live a *Little House on the Prairie* lifestyle. I had made dip candles at Camp Wolverine; that was the extent of my rustic farm experience.

Looking back over my interview notes, I was reminded that Martha claimed she had served Eleanore Roosevelt at the Purple Inn when she was in town to drop her daughter off at the Pinewood Camp. I wondered if there was any evidence of her visit.

Maurice Eby, a local historian and author of *The History of Brutus and Maple River Township,* writes:

The Pinewood Camp for Girls started on this property (Indian Point) in 1914 and existed until about 1939...Eleanor Roosevelt may have stayed at the Purple Inn in Brutus. She had supposedly brought her

[8]Scheer, Teva J. Our Daily Bread: German Village Life, 1500-1850. Adventis Press, 2010.

[9]Greenwood, Barbara. A Pioneer Sampler. Houghton Mifflin, 1995.

Purple Inn Dining Room   Brutus   Mich

BURT LAKE

PINEWOOD CAMP
BRUTUS, MICH.

daughter to stay at the Pinewood Camp. This would have been before she became famous.[10]

Ann O Thompson's Collection (1918-1926) of photographs of Pinewood Camp are accompanied by the following description: *This was a prestigious private summer camp for girls. The owner and director, Gertrude Tuttle, was originally from Hornell, NY and had been a teacher in Indianapolis. Ms. Thompson was believed to have been a counselor at the time. The subjects of the B & W photographs include camp scenes, group photos, lifesaving classes, swimming, horseback riding, canoeing, calisthenics, and a flag ceremony.*[11]

This trip to the library had proved to be a gold mine of research, but I was hungry, so I took a break to have a sandwich in the park. The day was warm and breezy, and I enjoyed watching vacationing families eat ice cream, spurring me to enjoy a delicious cup of my own.

I returned to continue work on a question I hadn't yet explored. A question that took me beyond my own family, beyond the Germans, beyond immigration to the natives of the land where my ancestors settled: Who were the Indians that Aunt Martha spoke of? The extent of my knowledge on indigenous culture was learned in the YMCA Indian Maidens troupe, started by Harold Keltner in 1926. Inspired by his relationship with Joe Friday, an Ojibwe Indian, he hoped to create a program to strengthen bonds between fathers and sons, with an emphasis on the role of the father as a teacher. In 1951, the program expanded to include mothers and their daughters.[12]

In our troupe, we met weekly with a handful of friends from the neighborhood, to make crafts, like leather pouches with beads and mats to sit on when camping. We went to YMCA camps where we tossed corn kernels into a campfire to pledge our commitment to be kind to one another and Mother Earth. We adopted new names based on nature: Mom was

---

[10]The History of Brutus and Maple River Township, Settled 1874, Emmet County, Michigan, https://www.emmet.migenweb.org/resources/brutus_history_maurice_eby.pdf

[11]Ann O Thompson's Collection (1918-1926), Archives Control Number: MS-90-247, Reading Room Archives of Michigan, https://researchworks.oclc.org/archivegrid/data/42424721

[12]Adventure Guides Program History, https://ymcaoc.org/adventure-guides-history/

Morning Glory, Laura was Cornflower, and I took the name of Sunflower. We earned patches for acts of service and marched in parades with our handmade ponchos. All in all it was an extremely positive experience for me, and promoted my love of nature. Perhaps this was why I became interested in learning more about the Native American culture. I have since learned how the program was culturally insensitive and even damaging to American Indians due to stereotypical practices and misunderstood rituals. Many YMCA programs have since acknowledged these kinds of problems and changed the name and focus.[13]

I wondered how American Indians fared in Brutus at a time when so much was changing in the growing United States, and at a time when so much displacement and forced assimilation was occurring for the American Indian tribes. Aunt Martha spoke offhandedly about Indian neighbors who sold baskets door to door. Where did they live? How did they live?

I found an article in the Petoskey Evening News, in May of 1953. The caption read, *Basket Weaving is Nearly a Lost Art — even among the Indians — but Mrs. Ida Shanaquet, of Route 2, Brutus, still devotes much of her spare time to the handicraft that was handed down to her by her mother, and grandmother. She is shown at work on a basket while her grand-daughter Elsie, 4, looks on.*

Ida learned how to make the black ash baskets from generational knowledge. She sold them for $4 to $7 to local souvenir shops. The article also mentioned Ida's sons who served in the military at that time.[14]

In the Emmet County Directory of 1900 an ad stated in big bold letters, "INDIAN BASKETS: We make a specialty of Indian Baskets, Bark and Quill Work, and we get the best because we buy directly from the Indians at their homes," for a store in the Petoskey area. The art of the indigenous was a commodity that also benefited the store owners who discovered its value with tourists. Unfortunately, the Indians were not usually paid a fair price for their time and talent. In Brutus, the Indians traveled by foot from door to door to sell their wares. They lived east of Brutus on Route 2, just a few miles from my great-grandparents home and farm.

[13]Carpenter, Adria. October 13, 2023, https://libnews.umn.edu/2023/10/playing-indian-a-retrospective-on-the-ymcas-indian-guides-program/

[14]Strohpaul, Petoskey Evening News, May 1, 1953, page 2.

Unlike my ancestors, the Indians in the area had a tried-and-true farming technique passed down for hundreds of years; they interplanted the *Three Sisters, Gitigaan.* Anishinaabe, *meaning the good humans,* in the Great Lakes region tended gardens using three seeds: corn, beans and squash. These plants complimented the others through support, nutrients and protection: corn provided stalks for bean plants to climb; beans provided nitrogen fertilizer; the squash shaded and kept weeds and pests out of the surrounding soil, helping to retain moisture. The plants did not fare as well when planted alone. However when planted together the fruit of the plants provided sustenance to entire communities, with balanced nutrition containing carbohydrates, protein, amino acids, vitamins and minerals. Indigenous plant wisdom evolved during pre-European contact, over 500 years of agricultural experience throughout the North American continent.[15]

The indigenous people of this land honored the three plants, told stories about them, and thanked their spirits through ceremonies as the sustainers of their communities. Had I known this as a young gardener, I would have asked Mom if I could plant a *Three Sisters Garden.* I reminisced on time spent tending a small starter garden, how much I'd learned about the soil and plants, gaining wisdom through the process from beginning to end.

Though I could find no information about a *Burn-Out* as Martha had briefly mentioned, I did find a book highlighting the experience of vacationers in the region titled, *In the Wake of the Topinabee: Cherished Memories of Lakeside Cottagers* by Arline M. Browne. In it she described the *Wayagamug Indian Play,* a performance that took place each summer starting in 1905 for five weeks daily, excluding Sundays. Here is a description of how the play based on Henry Wadsworth Longfellow's poem *The Song of Hiawatha* came to fruition.

> The Indians of the Algonquin Nation were living in the northern
> part of the Lower Peninsula when the French fur traders first came
> to America. They were called the Ottawa (Odawa) Tribe. The name
> Ottawa means trader. This tribe had migrated from the river in
> Canada which carries the same name. Another tribe of the same
> nation was the Ojibway or Chippewa, who lived on the north shore of
> Lake Huron. They were all friendly to the Frenchmen. In the first half

[15]Marsh, Emily Ph.D. The Three Sister of Indigenous American Agriculture. MLS, USDA National Agricultural Library, https://www.nal.usda.gov/collections/stories/three-sisters

of the 19th Century, Henry Schoolcraft was working with the Indians as a Government Agent at Sault Ste. Marie. He became interested in their folklore and had first-hand knowledge of their customs, having married a granddaughter of an Indian chief (Jane Johnston- Ojibwe). He kept very accurate records which came to the attention of Henry Wadsworth Longfellow, who was the first poet to reveal in such masterful yet simple style the wholesome philosophy of the Ojibway Tribe.[16]

The reenactment based on the poem, was first recorded on birch bark for Longfellow's children, whom the Indians loved and said, "The memory of our people will never die as long as your father's song lives, and that will live forever." Tourists took the dummy train, an engine pulling a few coaches, east to Round Lake from Petoskey. Canadian Ojibway tribal members had the main roles and taught Ottawa tribal members, living in the area, their parts. The set was minimal, but a grandstand was built, on which the audience could view the play near a *western style* village with white tipis. Costumes, or regalia, were no doubt authentic as displayed in a brochure. In the closing scene, the main character, Hiawatha, stood in a canoe as it disappeared into the sunset. The play lived on for eleven years and was sponsored by the G.R. & I. Railroad. It was said to have been as good as Broadway shows of the time.

Author Bill Dunlap, an Ottawa native who resided in Petoskey, was invited to participate in a similar Hiawatha pageant performed on the Petoskey High School football field as a youth in the thirties. The city manager Mac McDonald directed the play and offered to pay the adult actors $5.00 each and the children $3.50 each. This was a big deal! Yet the monetary gain wasn't the only benefit. In his book, *The Indians of Hungry Hollow* Bill shared: *The group of poor, half-hungry wretches that had begun rehearsals a few months before had vanished. In their place stood a vibrant, rejoicing, happy people. Working together and reaching for excellence had transformed us...Our eyes were opened that night to what our ancestors had always known about themselves. A wave of respect swept through us, washing away our shame as it went.*[17]

In my hometown a local English teacher directed a play every summer as

---

[16]Browne, Arline M. In the Wake of Topinabee. Hubbard Map Service, 1967.

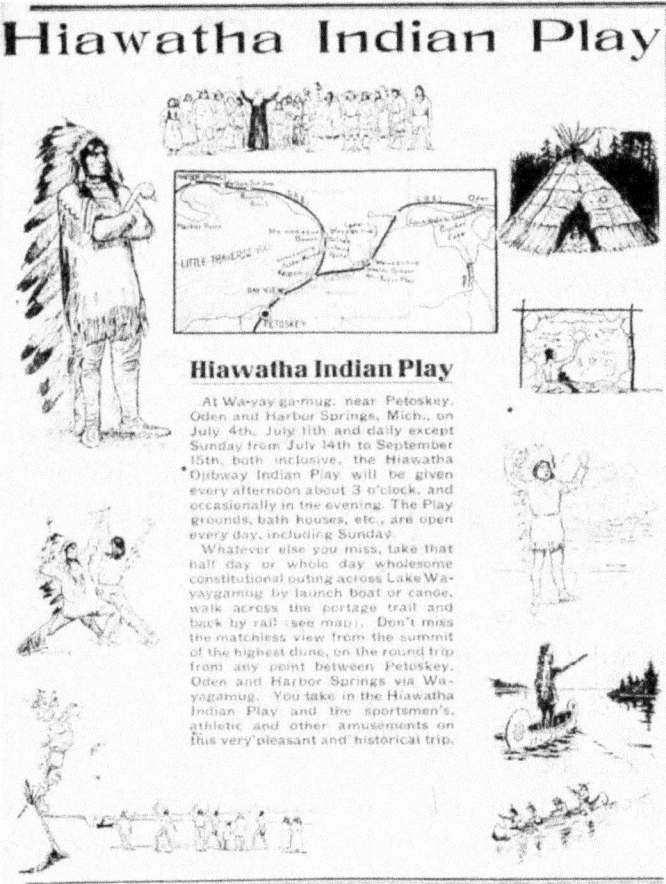

July 2, 1906 Petoskey Evening News advertisement

the founder of *The Lathrup Youtheatre*. For many summers my sister and I had the privilege of being a part of these shows. In fact, they were a highpoint during my childhood, since school was a struggle academically and socially. In my first role as a *Bluebell Flower* I wore large sky-blue petals draped from shoulder to waist with sewn sequins and a cute little hat. Mrs. Lamun, our director, wrote a letter of affirmation after the show:

> *Dear Julie Bluebell,*
>
> *Gosh I was proud of you! Your first time onstage and everything — and you did so well! I could hear you 'way back in the kitchen and you looked absolutely adorable. I hope you were proud of yourself and all your hard work. You earned all that applause! I hope you made some new friends, enjoyed working with the group, and, most of all, had fun! I enjoyed getting to know you and look forward to seeing you next summer.*
>
> *Sincerely,*
> *Jo Anne Lamun.*

Mrs. Lamun left a permanent mark on my life; because she believed in me, I learned to believe in myself. At the age of 11, I happened to see Mrs. Lamun at the grocery store when shopping with Mom during the spring. She said, "Julie, I think you are ready for a big part this summer!" My heart leapt with anticipation but I was shy and just smiled as I looked up into her bright eyes, to see if she really meant what she was saying. After the auditions, I happily discovered she did live up to her word. I was given one of the lead roles as *Nan*, and Laura played my twin. During a rehearsal, I was practicing my solo when one of the orchestra members said, "Can't she sing any louder?" I was so embarrassed and crumpled inside, wanting to quit. But Mrs. Lamun shushed him, and encouraged me to continue. I trusted her, and thus had the strength I needed to fight back tears.

By opening night, I had grown in confidence and courage; I sang with a blossoming stage voice. In subsequent years, I continued having prominent

[17]Dunlop, Bill and Marcia Fountain-Blacklidge. The Indians of Hungry Hollow. University of Michigan, 2004.

roles until the age of 14. I felt like a big deal when the local newspaper printed a photo of me as *Zinger,* the narrator and mime. Something about these experiences nudged me out of a shy-girl stage, and I fell in love with performing. These opportunities led to dance classes, a dance scholarship to Wayne State University, and a lifetime love of theater and performance.

Audiences young and old, attended the *Wayagamug Indian Play* out of curiosity or spectacle. Did these shows create positive cross-cultural relationships or did audience members leave believing the often called "red savages" should give up their ways and adapt? Was it all merely spectacle? Certainly they provided needed income in a society that was forcing the natives to assimilate. They could no longer depend on selling fur to the French; they could no longer sell fish or hunt as they had in the past; they could no longer live off the plentiful lands of their ancestors, not able to migrate in fall and spring seasons; they had been kicked off their lands due to failed treaty upon treaty. Fortunately, many tribes in Michigan were not forced to relocate west like most in the U.S. Over time they acclimated to western capitalism in part by selling hand crafts.

The 5:00 church bells chimed in downtown Petoskey; I realized I'd spent all day at the library. It was time to head back to the cottage.

Later in the week, Dave and I picked up the professional reproductions of the photos of Brutus from Bruce, and returned the originals to the Brutus Post Office to retrieve my driver's license. Then we drove to the Native American Art Gallery in Petoskey, where I purchased a few memoirs written by American and Canadian Indians.

With encouragement from Dave, I spent the rest of our vacation sitting on the deck, reading by his side. We had wonderful discussions. I shared what I was learning from indigenous voices, gleaning a bird's-eye view of what it was like to grow up in colonized America. The authors poetically depicted the brokenness, the shaming, and the loss of land, identity and dignity, yet also of their resilience. I was compelled to be a listener.

———————

As our cottage stay came to a close it was time to pack up and leave, which always caused sadness, but especially this time. I was leaving my ancestors and the beautiful place where they lived. I felt more at home in this place, than my own home in Anderson, Indiana. Even so, I left with an increased awareness and knowledge regarding the value of delving into history, my history.

Yes, I had found my people, those that shared my DNA, those that bravely transplanted their families in Northern Michigan to make a life for themselves and their faith communities. Yes, I had become aware of their uncanny commitment to survive in a small farming town, even after the loss of so many family members. Uncle Carl and Aunt Martha were determined to make the farming life work as brother and sister. And yes, I was so grateful for the sacrifices they made, that enabled me to grow up in a land of plenty. What surprised me, was a reacquaintance with emotions that had risen to the surface, forcing me to think deeper about loss. I had tapped into the voices of female ancestors who suffered in silence, who acquiesced, who carried on, spurring me to consider listening to my own voice.

part 2
autumn

There is no such thing as death. In nature nothing dies. From each sad remnant of decay, some forms of life arise ...
—Charles Mackay

to the city

Back to the rat race. I was teaching in a kindergarten classroom and Dave was back in seminary at Anderson University. Yet the recent discoveries were still fresh and exciting, distracting me as I tried to write my lesson plans. I needed more, questioned more, hoped to fill in the outlines with details that might have gone unspoken. I set up a time to meet with Aunt Mitzy, who lived in Detroit. Perhaps she too would open up about the past like her sister Martha. On Fall Break, I was able to get back to Michigan, to my childhood home in Lathrup Village, just north of Detroit, where my parents still resided. The drive from my parents' home to Aunt Mitzy's quaint brick bungalow in the city took 20 minutes. It had been a while since I'd visited, but Mitzy's home was instantly identifiable by two towering pine trees on either side of the front entryway.

While attending Wayne State University, I assisted Aunt Mitzy weekly, taking her grocery shopping, to the bank, and helping with household chores. She was legally blind, so I was happy to help. Even blind, she demonstrated the resourcefulness and grit I had begun to recognize in my ancestors. My role with Aunty Mitzy was to assist her — she was still determined to be the do-er. She inspired me. These were formative times; she loved me like I was her own at a time I had lost both grandmothers and longed for the wisdom and comfort of women in her generation. For this visit, I hoped to hear her unique perspective of growing up on the farm as the youngest sibling.

Once I arrived, I parked in the driveway and made my way to the side door that entered into the kitchen. I knocked hard a few times, to make sure she would hear, and in a few moments heard Aunt Mitzy questioning, "Who is it?" She couldn't see who I was through the window pane, but she knew my voice, and when she opened the door to welcome me she knew my frame, my touch, my fragrance. Indeed, despite her visual impairment, Aunt Mitzy amazed me as she zipped around her tiny kitchen preparing lunch with nimble fingers moving like seeing eye dogs. She had a solid routine, and knew exactly where to find things. A petite size 2, breasts smaller than my own, she wore a peach button-up sweater with a dainty floral scarf, cat-like glasses and pearl clip-on earrings. She belonged in a fashion magazine for 70+ women.

After a standard lunch of Campbell's Tomato Rice soup, a ham salad sandwich, and canned peaches with a dollop of mayonnaise on a bed of lettuce, we cleared the dishes and retired to the 12' by 12' living room. Mitzy sat in a blue and white upholstered rocker with swan-neck arms, and I on the yellow damask loveseat beside her.

"Aunt Mitzy, on my last visit to Indian River, I went to Petoskey and visited with your sister, Martha. It was so nice to see her. She made us dinner and was so kind to answer a bunch of questions about the Dieterich farm. She even opened up her old travel trunk and showed me old photos and news clippings! It was so fun! It's really opened up a huge interest for me in my history — particularly your generation."

Mitzy rocked her chair back and forth and fidgeted with a handkerchief as she listened, a subtle smile forming on her lips. "I am curious about your experiences, too! Could you tell me about some memories you might have of your childhood in northern Michigan?" I started digging out the legal-pad and pen from my backpack. As I was speaking Mitzy's subtle smile emerged into a huge grin, and she giggled shyly like a little girl.

She said, "You know once I moved to the city, I didn't think too much about my memories of the farm. It's been quite a while since I talked about it."

She sat silently for a minute, staring off in the distance as a blind woman does, then unexpectedly, perked up like a Chatty Cathy.

"Well, I don't know where to start. Life on the farm was just normal. I didn't know anything different. Brutus was a nice town. A nice community." She paused and then continued as she saw something in her mind's eye. "There was a special place in town named the Purple Inn. My sister Martha worked there as a waitress. There was a beautiful doll displayed in a glass case in the entryway, and as a young girl I wanted that doll so badly. On Christmas morning my brother Carl surprised me! I found the doll wrapped under the Christmas tree. I named her Dorothy; she was my favorite toy. That was very special, you know. We didn't have as many toys as kids do today. My sister Emma gave me a book she had purchased from Wagley's General Store by Gene Stratton Porter titled *A Girl of the Limberlost*." Mitzy popped up, and moved toward a bookshelf where somehow she found that precise book and handed it to me. I opened the front cover and read the inscription, *To Amelia, From Emma.*

She said, "You'll like it, it takes place in Indiana where you live, and it's all about nature."

I was touched, and immediately cherished this connection to the past. My past. "Wow! Thank you Aunt Mitzy, this is so generous of you! I will be sure to read it!" (Not only did I read it, I started a collection of Gene Stratton Porter books, visited her home and read her biography. It turned out that my old Aunt Mitzy and I were kindred spirits.)

After a few more memories, it seemed Mitzy was finding her rhythm. She was retrieving artifacts of memory that had been locked away for years. She got up again and invited me to follow her to the hall closet, across from the stairs to the attic, where she carefully pulled out a gift box tied with string. From inside she removed a small birth book wrapped in tissue paper, the size of a gift box for jewelry. She handed it to me, unable to read the handwriting herself. I carefully opened the cover and turned the delicate yellowed pages one by one. As I came upon handwritten memos, I read aloud the names and birthdates of Gottlieb's brother and sister in Germany and all of Gottlieb's children.

"Aunt Mitzy, this book has birthdates and names of your entire family! Who recorded all this information?"

She responded, "My aunt in Germany sent this book to my father as a gift. Then he and my mother and I recorded the details. I'd like for you to have this. You can carry on the family heritage."

Emotion welled in my chest. "Oh, Aunt Mitzy, this is precious! Are you sure?" I asked.

"Yes, Julie. Nobody has asked about these things in years and years. And I won't be around forever." She smiled that big little girl smile again. "And you are the family genealogist! Come, let's sit back down," she directed like a mother hen.

I followed her back to the living room where we sat and she continued her flow of memories, occasionally dabbing her watery eyes with her handkerchief. She shared a few details about the farm, but reminded me that as the youngest, she was not the most reliable source for information about the hard work of caring for farm and family.

Mitzy was different from her sister Martha in that she asked me questions about our lives in Indiana. She talked openly about missing Freddie, her late husband. Mitzy showed an interest in me — the way a grandmother would — and her questions were a reminder of the love that some women can share generationally. I thanked Aunt Mitzy once again for her generosity and love and asked how she was faring as a widow.

"I get by pretty well. Your parents come to help with house and a neighbor visits me regularly. I'm still active at church with the Ladies Aid Society. We make quilts for children overseas."

"That is wonderful. I wish I lived closer so we could visit more often."

After a period of awkward silence, Aunt Mitzy piped up, "Can I make you a cup of coffee?"

"Oh, I should probably get going, but thank you so much! Can I help you clean the dishes?"

She chuckled, "Oh no, I have plenty of time, dear." She pushed her diminutive frame up from the rocking chair and started into the kitchen. "Before you leave, let me pack up some homemade sugar cookies for you and your parents." I smiled and chuckled to myself. I never left her home empty handed. The Dieterich's take care of their own. We hugged goodbye and I promised to give her a call soon.

Later that week, Aunt Mitzy called my parents' house and asked if I could stop by before leaving town. I obliged, and arrived at her side door, where she was waiting, greeting me with a huge grin. "Come in, come in Julie!"

I asked, "What's up, do you have some good news?"

"Well..." she paused and looked toward me with childlike delight. "... prompted by your questions, I began to piece together my experiences growing up on the farm. You kind of inspired me! So, I recorded the stories on paper with my typewriter! Come sit down and you can read it back to me."

Since her eyesight was so poor, she couldn't read what she had written, and in fact, she wasn't aware the typewriter had run out of ink and the last three pages were blank. I read aloud what I could, and tried to decipher the last few pages by holding them up under a lamp to see the impression of the keystrokes on the pages. As I read her heart renderings, she took off her glasses, and nervously fluttered with her handkerchief, occasionally wiping tears from her soft blue eyes, just like her sister Martha.

> About father, Gottlieb:
> *"I remember my father as being a fun-loving, storytelling man who was musically inclined. He played the accordion and taught my sister, Emma, and I, to sing a German song about a dream, which regretfully I have forgotten the words. Emma and I had to sing this to friends and relatives who visited us. I remember when I was naughty, my father would put me over his shoulders and threaten to throw me into the pig pen."*

I got stuck on the word threaten, and wondered to myself: *Had he been drinking like Aunt Martha mentioned?*

"Did you lose your place, dear?" Aunt Mitzy noticed I was quiet.

"Oh, no, sorry." I continued reading.

> About mother, Magdalena:
> *"I remember my mother as a kind, quiet person. Her object was being a good homemaker and caring for her family. Being of the old-fashioned Mennonite ancestry, she dressed plainly and was very*

reserved. I loved her and remember her carrying on in spite of her suffering in her last days."

About brother, Carl:
"My only brother, Carl, was the oldest of my father's second family. When my father died, Carl took over the farm and cared for my mother, Emma and me. A few years later, when mother died, Carl cared for Emma and me and continued running the farm. That was hard work and he spent many long hours performing the farm chores. At that young age, I'm afraid I did not fully realize the sacrifices he made for me."

About sister, Matilda:
"Matilda, the second oldest, married Frank Schmidt when I was very young, so she was not living at home...In later years, after we finally had a car, Carl would drive over to Matilda's on a Sunday or Holiday. I remember the delicious meals Matilda would prepare. From their farm, they had a beautiful view of the distant hills and Crooked Lake. Matilda had a hard life, but she was a wonderful homemaker. Besides being a good cook, she was a good seamstress and made many beautiful quilts for her children and grandchildren...Matilda was a kind, sweet person. Her children Francis and Harriet were a great joy to her."

"Matilda had a hard life?" I asked out of curiosity.

"It's a very sad story, Julie. She was mistreated by her husband." Aunt Mitzy turned to face me, "No one should be subjected to such abuse."

"Oh. I'm so sorry Aunt Mitzy. How awful. You must have felt helpless."

"Yes...we did our best to speak highly of her at family gatherings, but she scoffed in unbelief." Mitzy sighed heavily. I heard the clock ticking on the mantel. I set the papers on my lap and moved my hands to my arms to keep warm. The room was cool. My mind raced. These women, these sisters had an incredible bond that must have sustained them through the many days and hours of suffering. They were stronger than I could ever be.

Aunt Mitzy broke the silence, "Would you like a glass of water?"

"Sure. That would be nice. Thank you!" I appreciated the moment to settle my anxious thoughts.

She whisked away to the kitchen and returned with two glasses full. I took a few sips and picked up where I'd left off.

> About sister, Martha:
> *"Martha, the third oldest of the second family, was always there when we needed her. She helped us in many ways, as well as financially. I remember one particular dress she bought me. It had a veil insert on the skirt and there was embroidered flowers on both the bodice and skirt. When she worked in Petoskey, she often would take the train to come home on her day off. When I saw her coming down the road, I would run to meet her."*

Aunt Mitzy interrupted with information I'd never heard; "Martha never dated, except for one guy who approached her with a marriage proposition, but she refused."

I supposed, *of course she refused, because after John died she was like one of the brothers of the family. She performed the boys' chores, left home at 16 to earn a living, and returned time and time and time again to care for the others. There was no time for a husband. She sacrificed her future with a husband for her family. I wondered, if this was the reason Martha had said it was "foolish" to go back to the farm after her sisters had moved on and married. Maybe Martha had regret. Wilson Snider had mentioned that townspeople thought Martha and Carl were a married couple.*

I continued reading,
> *"Martha did much to keep our family together. I am most grateful to her. Even at the age of 93, she said she wished she could come help me. Even in her later days with the infirmities of age, declining health, and loneliness, she is continuing on with courage. God bless her."*

Gottlieb Dieterich

Brutus

Mich

I turned to look at Aunt Mitzy with tenderness. "I think I'm beginning to understand how important your relationship with Martha and the others was to you."

Mitzy confided, "I felt comforted and cared for by my siblings. I grasped how vital they had been to my upbringing, to helping me through the tragedy of losing both parents by the time I had reached 11 years old."

I took another sip of water and swallowed hard through my tightened throat. Their loss was unimaginable. Thank God they had each other. And thank God I still had women like Mitzy and Martha in my own life.

Taking a cleansing breath, I carried on.

> About sister, Emma:
> *"Emma was the fourth member of the second family. She was the closest to my age being three years older. So we grew up together and I was always tagging along after her. I looked up to her. Whatever she did, I wanted to do too, but was afraid I couldn't measure up to her. Emma was more outgoing than I was. Our pleasures were simple ones. As young girls, we played with dolls. There were outdoor games. In the winter, there was sledding. When we were a little older, we received skis for Christmas. I soon broke mine by hitting a stump. There were always chores to do so there was not a lot of time for play. She had a lot of responsibility cast upon her when mother passed away...Emma was a fine homemaker, a good cook, an excellent seamstress, and loving mother. She even made me some beautiful dresses. I marveled at the many things she did, even gardening, and wondered how she managed. Just a few weeks before she went to the hospital and passed away, she insisted on coming over to bring me a birthday gift, in spite of a very bad chest cold. I owe her a debt of gratitude. She was indeed a big sister to me, loving and concerned."*
>
> *"This is a brief account of my wonderful family. I tried to cover some of the highlights. I may have missed some things, but I hope I haven't missed the most important things. I owe them much."*

Once she had finished thanking the family members for their impact on her life, Mitzy's memoir moved into a description of herself and personal experiences growing up on the farm.

"As the last child in the Dieterich family, I, Amelia Marguerite Dieterich Doletzke, was born September 4, 1914, in a country farmhouse one mile and a half east of Brutus, Michigan. Life on the farm was quiet, simple, but good, even though we did not have a lot of material possessions. There were wide-open spaces and the air was clean and fresh. We could enjoy the blue sky and various cloud formations. There was an apple orchard which bore fruit to enjoy. A garden produced many fresh vegetables. There were corn and grain fields and fields which produced hay for the livestock. There were two horses that did the farm work. Cows produced milk and beef to use and sell. Occasionally a chicken dinner was enjoyed. There was usually one dog that stayed outdoors and slept in a dog house. There were cats, most of them barn cats; only a few came to the house. A large barn housed farm tools, hay and grain, and sheltered the cows and horses. There was a pen for the pigs, and a chicken coop for the chickens. Only in later years did we own a car."

"There were always chores to do, so there was not a lot of time for play. Wood had to be brought in for the stove. Having no running water in the house, we had to pump the water and carry it into the house. Water had to also be pumped for the livestock. Chicken feed, usually corn, was spread; eggs had to be gathered. In the summer we often had to watch the cows when they were grazing so they would not get into areas that they should not graze in. Sometimes we would let them feed along the road. The cows had to be brought in from the pastures if they did not come by themselves. Sometimes this was done with the help of a dog. The cows had to be milked in the mornings and evenings. This was done by the older members of the family, brother Carl and older sisters. Emma did learn to milk the cows, but I as the youngest never learned. The milk was brought in the house to be separated. The cream was put into large cream cans, which was taken to town to sell. If there were young calves, they had to be fed milk."

"There were chores to help in the garden such as pulling weeds, and gathering the vegetables for eating and canning. Brother Carl did the heavy work on the farm. He spent many long hours in the fields and it was hard work in the days before modern machinery. Sometimes during haying time, Emma and I would get on the wagon. Carl would toll the hay onto the wagon and Emma and I would stomp it down so the wagon could hold more. One time the horses became frightened and started running away down the lane. But when they came into the barnyard, they got caught on the gate which stopped them. It was a frightening ride for us, but we were glad the horses could not get out on the road."

"We attended a country school in Brutus which was a mile and a half walk, nice in warm weather, but very cold in the winter with much snow. Occasionally we would get a carriage ride. At one time it was a two-room school, one for the lower and one for the upper grades. By the time I came along, it was just one room. I enjoyed school and was a fairly good student. I remember one time the bridge over the ravine near town washed out. Carl walked us to school and carried us across the swollen ravine. There was just one teacher over the one room school. We used to carry our lunch in a lunch pail. The lunch consisted of sandwiches—usually peanut butter, cookies or cake and an apple. In later days hot soup was provided and prepared by the older girls. During recess and lunch hour, we would play outdoors. The teacher would call one grade or class at a time to the front of the room to the front of her desk to go over their assignment. The class had to answer questions, recite or read. The whole room could hear what was said, so it was often difficult to concentrate on studying."

"I am grateful to my brother Carl, and my sisters, Martha and Emma, for seeing me through those early years."

As I finished reading those last words in the lamp light, I looked up at Aunt Mitzy who turned toward me with a questioning smile that seemed to seek my approval. I rested the pages in my lap and let out a satisfied, emotion-drenched

Brutus, Michigan Schoolhouse. Top photo Emma and Amelia are in the second row, students 9 and 10

For learning, virtue, truth and right,
"Tuebor" shout, God give us might,
Michigan, my Michigan!

Emmet County Public Schools

Teacher's Report to Parent

Pupil *Amelia Dieterich*

Grade *6th* District *1*

M. R. Twp. *Emmet* Co.

For school year 19*26*

Frieda E. Kaehler
Teacher.

A. M. HOOTMAN,
County School Commissioner

If You Wish to Succeed in Life

Be Cautious	Be Neat	Be Kind
Be Faithful	Be Honest	Be True
Be Industrious	Be Just	Be Courteous

The Michigan Education Company, Lansing, Michigan

TO THE PARENT OR GUARDIAN

This report will be sent you monthly. Your signature does not necessarily indicate your approval of the pupil's work, but it is an evidence of your having seen the record.

The attitude of your child toward his work is recorded on the preceding page. Impartial marks are always attempted; but should any dissatisfaction arise, you will do a great favor if you will consult with me directly and at once.

You are cordially invited to visit the school. You will then not only better understand our methods and aims; your presence will encourage both teacher and pupil. Home and school must dovetail their influence if we are to produce an American citizenship of the worthiest order.

Frieda Kaehler Teacher

SIGNATURE OF PARENT
I HAVE EXAMINED THIS MONTH'S REPORT

1st Mo. *Carl Dieterich*
2d Mo. *Carl Dieterich*
3d Mo. *Carl Dieterich*
4th Mo. *Carl Dieterich*
5th Mo. *Carl Dieterich*
6th Mo. *Carl Dieterich*
7th Mo. *Carl Dieterich*
8th Mo. *Carl Dieterich*
9th Mo. _____
10th Mo. _____

Certificate of Promotion
THIS CERTIFIES THAT

Amelia Dieterich

has completed the work of the preceding grade and is hereby promoted to the *7th* grade of the Public Schools.

May 27 19*27*

Frieda Kaehler Teacher

---

sigh. "Wow. Aunt Mitzy, this is tremendous. I really could imagine myself living on the farm! Though my romantic notions of farm life were dashed as you talked about the daily demands of chores you performed from sunup to sundown." She let out a burst of embarrassed laughter. To her it was just life. But she certainly understood my perspective.

I stood and placed the delicate typewritten pages into Aunt Mitzy's well-worn hands. "Your words are a beautiful tribute to your hard-working, perseverant family. I feel so proud to know the history of our roots. Aunt Mitzy, I feel proud to know you!"

She smiled and shrugged her frail shoulders, "Like I said, it was a simple life. I'm surprised but touched that you would take such a keen interest in our story."

Mitzy set the pages of her story aside and took a sip of water. I sat back down and leaned forward.

"So what happened after your parents had passed away?" Seeing if she had a few more insights and memories in her — and the energy to share them with me.

"Well, soon after Mom died, Carl, Martha, Emma and I moved to Grand Rapids to live with an older sister Christine and her husband Frank. I went to school there while the others worked as maids at the Waters Mansion. I was teased at school because of my long braids and farm-made cotton dresses, so I decided to cut my hair short to fit in. Christine took me shopping to buy new clothes. I was so incredibly grateful for her. Carl missed the farm terribly and moved back Up North a year later. Then Martha and I joined him. In northern Michigan, I lived with my sister Mollie and graduated from Petoskey High School. For a while I worked as a waitress at Jesperson's family café."

"I love Jesperson's," I exclaimed. We go every summer for a basket of breaded whitefish, fries, and home-made strawberry rhubarb pie ala-mode!"

Grabbing a taffy from the candy dish on the end table, I asked, "When did you move to the Detroit area?"

Mitzy pushed her glasses up as if it would help. She responded, "In 1942, I moved to Detroit where I lived with your grandparents, Emma and Edgar (Hilpert) to help after the birth of their third child, Kathleen. They took me in like a member of their own family in the crowded quarters of their small home. They extended their hospitality for a year or more until I decided to move downtown, into my own apartment. I remember that little apartment was so small; and it had only one window. But I felt proud of myself, you know, for being on my own. Fortunately, I had found a dependable job working for Michigan Bell as an accounting clerk. And I joined Holy Cross Lutheran Church; that's where I met your Uncle Fred!"

She beamed. I glanced at their wedding photo on the mantel. Aunt Mitzy was a widow. I could tell she missed her "Freddie" terribly.

"Uncle Fred was a good man, Aunt Mitzy. You must miss him a lot." I tried to empathize.

"I think about him every morning when I pour one cup of coffee instead of two. It's not easy being alone." She replied, moving her trembling hands to her mouth, restlessly.

"I'm sorry Aunt Mitzy. Thank you for your honest reflections." We both stood up and I gave her a hug. She felt delicate and small, as if I could break

Amelia's graduation photo

Waters Mansion in Grand Rapids
where Emma and Martha worked

CERTIFICATE OF PROFICIENCY

AWARDED TO

For typewriting _____ words a minute for fifteen minutes according to International Contest Rules

BY

PETOSKEY HIGH SCHOOL

In Testimony Whereof we have affixed our names this _____ day of _____ ____ at Petoskey, Michigan.

her bones if I squeezed too hard. Then she turned to feel for the typewritten papers she had written. She picked them up and handed them to me.

"This is for you."

She had called me a genealogist. She had said no one had asked her about these things in years. She had lost her eyesight but not her memories. Now they were in my hands, as were Martha's. I was beginning to see that this interest in my history was more than a personal curiosity or hobby. I was beginning to feel responsible to pass on her words, our family story, to the next generation. These women were entrusting their stories to me.

I didn't want to leave, but the daylight faded fast. I promised her words would appear in a book someday. She expressed appreciation for my time and interest in her life as a simple farmgirl.

I drove away glancing in the rearview mirror. She stood in the driveway waving goodbye. I returned the gesture even though she couldn't see it.

It was my turn to wipe a tear away.

home

I was hungry and tired. The beat of the pavement on Southfield Freeway lulled me into a trance. Being with Aunt Mitzy stirred a forgotten sadness I had buried. I missed Grandma Emma. I wouldn't ever be able to talk to her about her childhood memories. It was a feeling I couldn't fix, which made the sadness greater. Emma died from heart failure at the age of 73 when I was just 13; before I knew to care about the details of her life.

I desperately hoped to glean information about Grandma at my parents'. Since they had cleaned out my grandparents' home after my Grandpa Edgar was no longer able to care for himself, I wondered if I could dig up anything that could help piece together her story.

My parents' classic two-story brick colonial childhood home was the only place I remembered living before moving-out during college. I didn't move out by choice so much as by necessity. Grandpa Edgar was not coping well living in the nursing facility. After Grandma Emma died, Grandpa's mental health declined to such an extent that he needed to be hospitalized after attempting suicide. Medication brought some relief, and 24-hour care provided some peace of mind, but living at the nursing home caused Grandpa Edgar overwhelming anxiety. It was a constant source of stress for my father. Dad believed our home would be a better option for Grandpa, so he and his brother Arnold, who lived in Florida, decided that Dad would take on the responsibility of caring for their father full time.

The change in living conditions seemed appropriate, even though it meant a major change for me. Grandpa moved into my bedroom, so I moved in with a family friend as a boarder. Dad's solution to house Grandpa gave Dad a purposeful job and a financial solution to unemployment. Mom became the main bread-winner working full-time for Lutheran Special Education Ministries. Dad was out of work, fired — (forced to resign, more accurately) — having found the corporate environment more frustrating than fulfilling. His boss dictated, "Either you leave, or I'll make it hell for you to work here." It already felt like hell, so Dad resigned and searched for new work. But finding a new job in his fifties that would pay him commensurate with his experience didn't pan out. Instead, he became a day-trader on the stock market and took care of Grandpa Edgar, who we tenderly called "Gramps."

Pulling up in the driveway, slowly over the ditch pipe bump, which could destroy a car's axles if taken too fast, I could see Dad working vigorously on a ladder outside the front bay window, chipping away at peeling paint on the wooden window frames. He wore his standard Kmart loafers, a pair of blue pants stained with paint smears, and a white T-shirt under a half-buttoned flannel shirt.

"Hello Dad! I'm back! I had a nice visit with Aunt Mitzy." I paused and surveyed the house front. "How's it going?"

"Hi Julie," he called. "Not bad," he turned to look at me from the ladder. Flecks of paint spotted his shoulders, face and hair like snow. "The work on this house never ends, Julie! And the guy I hired last year to glaze these windows did a terrible job, so I have to do it again myself." Dad was always doing (or re-doing) something on the house; and the work that others did never (never) met his standards. So he worked. And worked. "I'm glad you had a good visit with Mitzy. I'm sure she appreciated seeing you." He wiped his forehead with the back of his left arm. "Hey, could you do me a favor?"

"Sure, what do you need, Dad?"

"Can you get me that pack of cigarettes on the red bench on the porch?" he asked.

"Aw, Dad. Come on. When are you going to quit?"

"Soon enough, toots. But not today." He turned to get back to work and I dutifully found the pack of cigarettes and tossed them up to him.

I stood outside for a while and watched him. I noticed the deep etches in his forehead glistening with sweat. His hair was whiter than I recalled since my last visit. I spent a lot of time worrying about Dad. As I grew up, dinner times were often spent listening to him obsess about unfair treatment at work or stupid drivers on the way to work and home from work or his never-ending to-do lists fixing cars or the house and yard. We caught glimpses of joy when he could set his burdens aside to play with us for a few minutes after dinner, but later when the peculiarities of being a man in a house full of women would overwhelm him, he'd disappear to the basement. When he lost his job and couldn't find work, depression set in. At times, thinking about it, I broke down in sobs hoping and praying Dad could find contentment. Cigarettes, coffee and alcohol seemed to be some of his only relief.

I proceeded into the house, pulling the door closed tightly behind me. Inside the living room Grandpa Edgar was taking a cat nap in the velvety green chair next to the fireplace. These days, he slept more and more. His once tall slender body now slouched over, boney and bent from years of work and stress. He still had a full head of neatly combed silver hair — more hair than my dad — and wore a handsome plaid shirt with a gray cardigan sweater for warmth. I stared for a minute, remembering the times Laura and I had combed his hair while he sat comfortably in that same chair. I'm not sure how we got the notion to offer such a bold act, but we knew it brought him happiness.

I continued on quietly past Gramps so as not to wake him, and found Mom cooking dinner in the kitchen. She was still in her work clothes: a smart office outfit, with nylons and painted toe nails. She had kicked off the one-inch navy heels and was standing in her stocking feet. Her lipstick had worn off, but she still looked put together and lovely, with her distinctive and timeless salt and pepper pixie cut.

"Hi Mom, do you need any help?" I asked.

"Sure, you can peel the potatoes. Thanks." She let out a weary sigh. "It sure is nice to have you home this week; to have you all to ourselves!" Mom smiled, yet her eyes looked tired.

"It's my pleasure Mom!" I replied with a genuine desire to help, unlike my immature 15-year-old self that would have balked. The kitchen was small, so we stood side by side, talking about our day. I relished time as an adult with Mom, and could communicate with her about most things, unlike during teenage years when I hid truths about my life. I shared enthusiastically what I'd been learning about the family history.

"Mom, do you know where I might find information about Grandma Emma and her childhood?" I inquired.

"Oh your father tucked away documents in various hiding spots around our house: check the dresser on the back porch, I think the hall cabinet at the top of the stairs may have some boxes, and if you're really brave you might look under the beds."

"Thank you Mom! It's a good thing Dad is a pack rat!" I snickered. Mom remained silent. Dad's obsession with hoarding was not a laughing matter for Mom. It would follow my dad to his grave.

After dinner, I sorted through stacks of memorabilia housed in a dresser oddly placed in the back sunroom. I turned on the overhead light. My first discovery lay innocently in a stack of saved greeting cards in the top dresser drawer. A dried rose fell to the floor as I pulled a note out of an envelope addressed to Edgar Hilpert. I had found a love letter from my grandmother, age 22, to her boyfriend Eddie. I debated whether to read the sacred text, but couldn't stop myself, unfolding seven yellowed pages. As I began to read the romantic musings, it dawned on me that Grandma and Grandpa, and Dave and I, shared similarities in our courting relationships.

My grandparents met through a mutual friend, as did Dave and I. They wrote sappy love letters to each other and sent them in perfumed envelopes through the mail; we too passed love notes (but without the perfume), between classes at W.S.U. Grandma listened to love songs that reminded her of Eddie; I too listened to ballads that reminded me of Dave. Whereas she listened to *Speak to me of Love* by Greta Keller and *I'll Never Have to Dream Again* by Isham Jones, I was listening to *Pictures of Love* by the Cure or *With or Without You* by U2.

Reading on, I sensed Emma's insecurity, for she wrote, "I have been wondering why you think I should deserve so many things as you wished me. Don't you think I am like every other girl?" Honestly, I too felt insecure as a young woman as I compared myself to others, and wondered why Dave was so kind to me, writing poems that likened me to a pure-white rose.

Knowing Emma was human, fallible, like me, brought a profound sense of comfort. I didn't feel pure like Dave described. As a people-pleaser, I valued the opinions of others more than my own. Before Dave came along, I believed my role as a female in a dating relationship was to keep a boyfriend happy, meeting his needs and disregarding my own.

Since adolescence, destructive thoughts had moved in and out of my mind like unexpected dark clouds, sometimes in dreams, sometimes around moments of conflict, sometimes when I looked in the mirror and I saw all the eyelashes that seemed out of place, and pulled them out. As a young person, and even into adulthood, anxieties would often grip me and try to define me. It would take an accepting and wise female therapist to help me begin to think differently.

As I sat on the floor in the back sun room of my parents' home, I wondered if Grandma Emma had had similar thoughts. If she had struggled as I had. If

Mr. Edgar Hilpert
9364 Stoepel ave.
Detroit, Mich.

she had ever been able to meet with a therapist and receive wise counsel. Not likely. I wondered if Emma discovered her worth apart from her relationship with Grandpa. I put the letter back into the envelope.

I pulled out an old shoebox and sat down on a white wicker couch, to peruse stacks of faded color photos. Grandma looked happy. I drifted back in time to visits at Grandma and Grandpa's house as a child. Grandma's collections sparked a fascination for beautiful things. I loved her porcelain floral tea cups displayed on a cherrywood shelf my father had built. On occasion we could choose one to have a cup of tea with cookies. Grandma regularly invited us into her bedroom to count collected pennies with our birth-year dates. She stored them in pill bottles tucked away in a dresser drawer next to colorful beaded necklaces. Emma also collected dolls of all sizes, not as toys to play with, but as treasures to care for. One large doll with lovely auburn hair sat in a bedroom chair. Others were wrapped in tissue in boxes under her bed. She unwrapped each one, showing me and Laura how she had sewn their outfits and undergarments, brushed their hair, and put on their jewelry. I could tell these dolls were special to her, nearly living.

If we weren't looking at one of Grandma's collections, we were going on tours in her multi-colored rose garden, or listening to records on her big hi-fidelity stereo. On one particular visit as she was babysitting us, I remember feeling animated by the Spirit while listening to Handel's *Hallelujah Chorus*. I danced with twirls and leaps on the blue shaggy carpet in front of a large picture window, glancing at the flittering reflection. I felt happy and free, like a butterfly in a garden. It was one of my first memories of truly dancing; a moment of pure worship.

A focus on worship and prayer was central to my Grandma Emma and Grandpa Edgar. When Laura and I spent the night, we would overhear Grandma and Grandpa praying together, praying for us. This was not a perfunctory bedtime ritual for them. No, it was a heartfelt commitment to their belief that with God all things were possible and that the hand of God was active in our daily lives. They faithfully attended a local Lutheran church where Laura and I would accompany them. We loved going because on the way home we always visited McDonalds.

Sometimes, though, while sitting next to Grandma in church or watching her look out the kitchen window when doing dishes, she seemed sad. Once

I caught her with tears glistening down her cheeks. I asked if she was ok, and she turned and said with a smile, "Oh, don't you worry about me!" Then she dried her wrinkled hands on a calico apron and enfolded me in a warm embrace; I felt relieved in the comfort of her soft breasts. But at her funeral I couldn't stop crying; for her and for me.

I missed Grandma Emma. Why did she have to die so young, before I had the chance to talk with her as an adult woman? The intensity of loss had lessened, yet I wanted to know how to fill the longing stuck in my heart; an unsettled ache, an unfinished song. I shivered in the unheated space of the sunroom, and moved inside to find out more about the Emma others had known so well. Grandpa was again sitting in the green velvet chair with a blanket on his lap. I pulled out my legal-pad and pencil. I wasted no time.

"Gramps, can you tell me what Grandma Emma was like when she was younger?" I asked, peering into his eyes to see if I could spark a memory.

"Yeah." This was a common response from Gramps to just about any question. This man was more like a child than the grandpa who once upon a time would take me and my sister for rides on his riding mower. I thought maybe that would be the end of his response, but he surprised me and continued. He first commented on her appearance, "She was nice looking, pleasant." He looked up to the ceiling with a sweet smile, as if he could see her, and then looked back at me and gave me a nervous chuckle. "Emma was good with her hands; an accomplished seamstress. She made dresses for herself and Kathleen. And she was a gardener; she loved her roses."

"I remember her taking me on a tour of the rose garden. Gramps, you liked to garden too! How nice that you shared this hobby," I commented. He nodded.

"You know, most people thought of her as a good cook. She took pride in being organized, and was exceptional at making all kinds of pies!"

"And I'll bet you loved those pies, Gramps!"

He responded, "Uh huh," and offered nothing more. I pushed on.

"Gramps, can you tell me how you and grandma met?" He smiled and sat up straighter. His tender blue eyes shined in the soft lamp light.

"We met at St. John's Evangelical church... through a mutual friend. I would pick her up in my Model A and take her bowling, or to Belle Isle to see the flowers." He paused and smiled a genuine smile. "Sometimes we went to the movies." He lost himself in a memory and then proceeded while I scribbled notes on my legal pad.

"I enjoyed making your grandmother laugh. I gave her roses, Christmas ornaments... a diary. We went out for walks in the moonlight. When we first got married, on June 1, 1935, we lived with my folks, upstairs, in the house I grew up in. 9366 Stoepel Ave, Detroit, Michigan." Grandpa got quiet and as I looked up from my legal pad, I saw that he had dozed off. I stared out the front window as neighbor children squealed while playing on the sidewalk. I hoped to someday have kids of my own.

I gave Gramps a moment to rest, then, not to be deterred, jarred him awake, "Gramps?" I gave a gentle tap on his shoulder and he opened his eyes wide. "Gramps, I've been doing a lot of research about the Dieterich farm. Once Grandma moved down state, did she get back up to the farm much?"

Grandpa lifted his stooped head and wiped a drip off the end of his nose. His large hand trembled unnaturally as he pushed his glasses back into place. He replied, "We traveled up to the farmhouse every summer as a family. Your grandma liked to go Up North. She spoke to her brother and sisters in Dutch German. I liked to go fishing on Burt Lake. We would take the drive from Harbor Springs to Mackinaw as a ritual. She and Amelia and Martha would talk every week on the phone."

"Do you remember what they would talk about? I would have loved to have been involved in those conversations."

"Oh, you know. Girl stuff," Gramps replied with a smile. "Sharing recipes, talking about things going on and looking out for one another."

"Thank you Gramps! I bet you miss your Emma." He nodded and chuckled a bit. "She was a special lady!" He smiled at me and adjusted his position in the green chair and I took that as my signal that he was finished chatting, so I turned my attention to my father to see what memories I could coax out of him.

Dad was sitting in the dining room with the lights low, listening to smooth jazz music, his after-dinner routine. I wanted to be sensitive, and wasn't sure if he'd feel comfortable answering questions. I recalled Dad coming home from the hospital after Grandma Emma had just died. His eyes swelled with tears, as he said, "My mom has gone home to be with the Lord." Then he hugged me for a long-long time as we both cried. I'd not seen or heard him cry like that before. It felt like I held him up with my 13-year-old body.

I pulled up a chair to sit at the table covered with a golden table cloth. Mom creatively decorated the center with a cornucopia of fall-colored dried flowers.

"Dad?"

"Hmm?" he responded; eyes closed.

"Do you have a minute to share a few memories about Grandma Emma?" His sincere smile encouraged me to turn to the next blank page in my legal pad.

He began, "Sure. Are you still working on the family history?"

"I am. I'm on a mission, Dad." I smiled and laughed nervously. On the stereo Toots Thielemans, one of Dad's favorites, played a smooth mellow harmonica. Dad spent a lifetime in love with jazz. Every summer he took us to the Montreux-Detroit Jazz Festival at Hart Plaza downtown on the riverfront. I followed Dad around like his mini-shadow as he bounced from one stage to another, teaching me about the instruments, the syncopated rhythms, the soulful improvisation. Dad once taught me how to slow dance listening to Miles Davis's *Round Midnight.*

Dad set his beer bottle on the table and began. "Well...My mother was a perfectionist, but also resourceful. She made her own clothes, and was conscientious about her appearance. When I was little I called my mom the 'prettiest woman in the world!' From my child-like perspective, this made her proud and happy. She was my advocate," he got quieter, "especially when it came to dealing with my father."

I looked over to Grandpa, who was oblivious. Dad continued.

"She was also melancholy. I think she dealt with depression; she felt insecure that she had only finished eighth grade. But when people were coming over to our house, she was all lit up, and put on her best face. She kept a journal of the home-cooked meals prepared for family and friends, what they liked, and didn't like, could and couldn't eat. At Christmas time, she made dozens of different kinds of cookies. Of course, I loved every one and offered to sample them before the guests arrived."

Dad took a sip of beer. He had cleaned up before dinner and put on a navy crew neck sweater. His aged wiry hair and eyebrows were messy, but he was tan, and handsome with a thick Tom Selleck style mustache. I noticed he looked more like his mom, with round expressive lapis lazuli eyes. Deep like an ocean.

More secrets revealed. Grandma dealt with depression, before Prozac. I could relate, and I think Dad could too. I pondered our shared experience; it must run in the family. The dark cloud that descends and doesn't blow away, even when days should be happy and full of wonder.

I pressed him further, "Dad, do you know why Grandma had depression?"

"I'm not sure, Julie. I know she had a difficult relationship with her father. She didn't talk about this much, but I remember hearing she was afraid of him."

"I'm sorry, Dad."

There was a long silence. I could hear him breathing through his nose. His chest rose and fell. He shook his head and rubbed his forehead, like his head hurt. Another sip of beer.

I changed the subject. "Do you remember visiting the farm as a child?"

He glanced up and smiled, looking like a boy. "Sure, I remember going Up North to the farm. Uncle Arnold would stay for the entire summer, but I would go for a week. We had space and time to roam the fields, scare the cows, play make-believe in the barn, read dirty magazines in the attic, and gather eggs from the chicken coop... Uncle Carl would take us for rides on the tractor. Carl was shy and had funny mannerisms. And he always wore overalls. Never saw him without those overalls — even at church." He laughed. "He was self-educated and well-read; a very moral God-fearing man." Dad took another sip of Stroh's. "They were simple people. We usually made the rounds to visit Aunt Matilda, Aunt Molly, and Aunt Martha. But my favorite memory was playing with Uncle Carl's farm dog, Buster."

He took the last sip of his beer and stood up. I followed suit. Then, we hugged while I counted his breaths, like sidewalks around my heart. It was an adult connection. I understood something deeper about Dad, about his own relationship with loss.

"Julie, I'm going to head downstairs to work on weathering a model general store I just put together for my train exhibit. Thanks for writing down all this information about our family history." He turned to go and gave me his loving farewell, "See ya' later toots!" I loved it when he called me toots.

"Thanks for talking, Dad." It felt good to know Dad valued my work.

I headed upstairs to my childhood bedroom, the walls adorned with the

Carl and Martha with Gary, Arnold and Kathleen on the farm

same yellow floral-patterned wallpaper from years ago. Like Mom suggested, under the bed I found several boxes. In a shirt box covered in dust I found a curious document coming apart at the fold lines. With the hands of a surgeon, I unfolded it on the bed and tried to decipher the German words. It appeared to be a baptismal document from 1860 for Christena, Gottlieb's first wife. I couldn't believe a 150-year-old record had survived a trip across the ocean, the journey to Canada, to Northern Michigan, to my grandparent's home, and subsequently to my parent's home. The family story was coming full circle, starting with the discovery of Christena's grave, and now marked by finding this record of her baptism. It was evidence that our family indeed came from Murrhardt, Germany as Aunt Martha had said. A precious artifact of truth. I folded the document and returned it to the box next to Grandma Emma's baptismal and confirmation certificates. That dusty box was a gold mine!

I moved to the hall, remembering paper stuff had been tucked into a built-in cabinet that also contained bath towels and sheets. I opened the cabinet and stood on a chair to peer past the linens to see what I could find. Under a stack of souvenir vacation brochures and maps, I discovered a faded blue stationery box tied with string, just like Aunt Mitzy had done to secure her artifacts. I carefully pulled it out and closed the cabinet doors. I set the box on the carpeted floor, knelt before it, and opened it slowly. Inside were letters I couldn't read. They were in German, and the return addresses were in Germany!

"Whoa! This is so cool!" I said out loud.

My Grandma Emma was the recipient of these letters. How could I find out what they said? I recalled one of Dave's professors was from Germany. Maybe he could translate them for me when I returned to Indiana.

At the bottom of the box, I found Gottlieb's naturalization document, confirming his American citizenship on February 15, 1895. I was suddenly acutely aware that I existed because of Gottlieb's decision and determination to immigrate to America, build a log home, a church, start a family, and raise 11 children as a homesteader. I felt conflicted; both nascent anger for the ways Gottlieb's behavior may have negatively affected my family, as well as gratitude for his profound sacrifices.

Back in the cabinet, I checked for more boxes. Under a pile of yellowing doilies, I pulled out a shoe box, containing sympathy cards to my

Königreich Württemberg.

Neckar-Kreis. Oberamt Backnang.

Parochie }
Gemeinde } *Mürrhardt*

Auszug aus dem Taufregister.

Im Jahre Ein Tausend Acht Hundert *fünfzig*

den *achten Juli* wurde in der

Wimberg Gemeinde *Mürrhardt*

den
8. Juli
1860.

ehelich geboren und am *11. Juli* getauft

Christian

Eltern: } *Josef Völkas, ... Maria Elisabeth geb. Wagner von Wagershofen*

Taufzeugen: }

Die Treue dieses Auszugs

bezeugt:

Mürrhardt den *12. Aug.* 188*1*

Königl. Württemb. *Diaconat* **Amt**

Klaidwae.

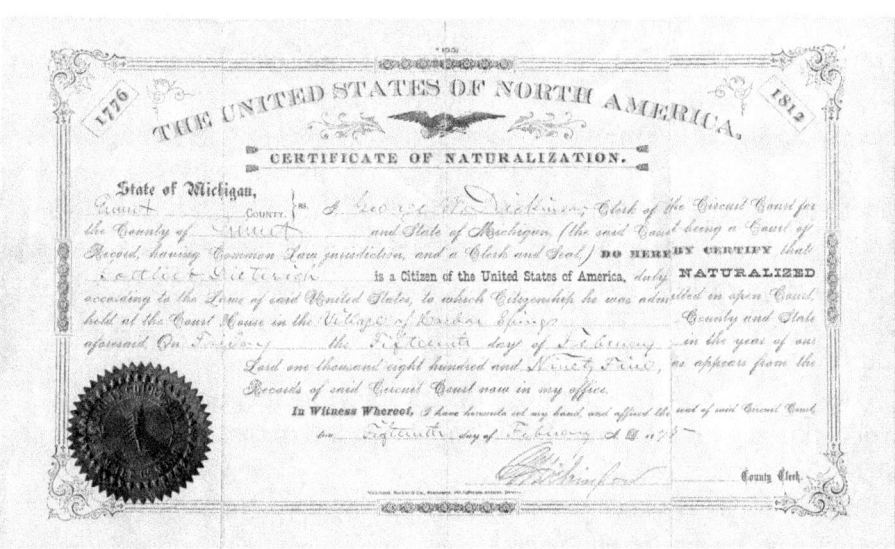

grandparents after the loss of their daughter, Kathleen. The family rarely spoke of Kathleen. All I knew was that my dad's younger sister had passed at a young age. Other than that, she was a ghost. As I looked through the cards, I found a letter from Kathleen to her parents while she was away at college. She began the letter by describing the extreme anxiety, paranoia and confusion about her safety. As I turned the pages, the words got larger, eventually becoming undecipherable circular scribbles. There was page after page of scribbles. My heart raced; my face flushed; I felt panicked. I didn't want to ask, but had to. *What happened to Kathleen?*

I decided to show the letter to Mom, privately, and make my inquiry. It would be too hard to approach Dad. Mom was still in the kitchen, working on lessons for next week's classes.

I asked with hesitancy, "Mom, I found this strange letter from Aunt Kathleen. What happened to her?"

Mom touched my arm and looked at me with seriousness, "Have a seat, Julie." I looked into her empathetic eyes for understanding. Mother was a strong woman, and I always trusted her to tell me the truth.

She quietly and gently exposed the secret, opening a moment in history the family had locked up years before. "Your dad didn't want you to worry, so he hasn't ever shared this with you...his sister Kathleen died of a mental illness. She died in a hospital room where she was being treated for paranoid schizophrenia. It was the summer we were to get married. It almost stopped the wedding, but the pastor encouraged us to go ahead; but it was extremely difficult."

Gripped with disbelief and shock, I dropped my faint head into my hands, held up by weakened elbows on the table. *Suicide.* Mom went on, "Grandma Emma grieved quietly. For nine years she couldn't shed a tear." I thought about Grandma's doll collection; all the time she'd put into making them beautiful. Perhaps one of them belonged to Kathleen. Perhaps one of them represented Kathleen to Grandma.

I was shaken. Paranoia? Schizophrenia? Hospitalization? This was a punch in the gut. I wondered about myself. My own battles with anxiety. My thoughts started to derail, so I redirected myself to asking questions: "What was Kathleen like?" I wanted to know more about her life, rather

FROM KATHY TO
Mother

To Mothe
From KATHY
I love pou Mother

than talk about her death.

Mom answered cautiously, wanting the details to reflect an accurate picture. "She was studying in college to be a teacher. I remember Kathleen as being somewhat shy, but very bright, and she had a lovely smile. She was in Girl Scouts for many years; Grandma Emma was the scout leader. They were very close. At first she went away to college. She cleaned people's houses to earn some income. But with the onset of the illness, she wasn't coping with being so far from home, so she returned to attend school locally. Faith was an important part of her life, but even so, the intense anxiety and paranoia caused immense mental suffering."

The burden of this secret was too great. I wanted to give Dad another hug, but thought, *maybe I should keep this secret too.* I was thankful for Mom's bravery and strong voice. I was thankful the family persevered, but I was scared. Could this illness strike me too?

Mom seemed to intuitively know my thoughts. She got up from the table and prepared some chamomile tea. When she handed me the mug, she gently put her hand on mine, as if to say, "You'll be ok, Julie."

Later that evening, in my childhood bedroom painted white with blue trim by Dad years before, I curled up like a baby, pulling a quilt Mom had made up to my chin and around my shoulders, tucking myself in. I began to cry and pray. "God, help me make sense of all this pain. Why all this mess? Why is our family so broken? Why?"

part 3: winter

the sound of a water jar
cracking on this icy night
as I like awake
—Matsuo Basho

to the doctor

That winter, I couldn't stop thinking about all I had uncovered. Like peeling bark off a dying tree, I had stripped the pretense and perfection, revealing our embarrassing familial nakedness. Dave was a good listener and comforted me as I told him the truths, but feelings of panic would regularly interfere with daily activities. I cried frequently, and felt a heaviness on my mind and mood for weeks. I was afraid. I feared mental illness, and was angry that it had the power to kill. Would I be next? I shared my struggles with a few of my friends — wives of some of Dave's friends from the Seminary, who suggested I talk to my doctor. I agreed. But I also decided to learn more about mental illness, the history, causes and treatments for myself.

Schizophrenia, in the 18th century would have led to persons living on the streets, in asylums or jails. Persons afflicted with this disease at that time would have been written off as "insane." During the 19th century, the illness was recognized as psychosis and patients began to receive care in hospitals, but it was still widely misunderstood, and feared. In the 20th century doctors began experimental and invasive treatments such as "insulin coma, Metrazol shock, electro-convulsive therapy, and frontal leukotomy." Finally, by the 1960's patients were being treated successfully with neuroleptic medications and released, yet many had poor post-treatment follow-up and fell through the cracks, often to relapse. It wasn't until the 1990's that more effective "antipsychotic agents" began to positively support the health of persons identified as schizophrenic.[18]

---

[18]Tueth, M. J. Schizophrenia: Emil Kraepelin, Adolph Meyer, and Beyond. J Emerg. Med. 1995 Nov-Dec;13(6):805-9. doi: 10.1016/0736-4679(95)02022-5.

Aunt Kathleen passed in the era when medical advancements were just starting to become effective. As I considered my own fears, I reasoned that if I were to show signs of the illness, I'd have better options for treatment. Even so, I wrestled with obsessive thoughts.

My doctor prescribed me an antidepressant, saying, "There's no shame in treating a chemical imbalance in the brain, just like there is no shame in taking insulin for diabetes." As I began my regime of medicine, the looming sense of panic and pervasive sadness began to lift.

Nature had always been a place to escape, to sort out the difference between imagination and reality, a place to fully engage my five senses without having to think so hard, a place to allow God to lead me back to center. So I took a walk at a nearby preserve where I came to the conclusion that because life is precarious, I could suffer from any number of genetic predispositions, including diabetes which also ran in my family, so I might as well do the best I can to have a healthy lifestyle and let go of controlling my future — mind, body, and spirit. It was a step in the right direction.

As I found my footing again mentally and emotionally, I was once again able to think about the family history. I wanted to start with the letters from Germany. This was a part of the family story that no one could really tell me about. These artifacts were like a code that needed to be broken in order to peer into the past. I couldn't break the code myself; I needed help. I had to know what the letters from Germany said. Who were they from?

Dave helped arrange a time for me to meet with his professor Dr. Walter Froese. Dr. Froese was willing to translate the letters and asked me to meet him in his tiny office overlooking "the valley" on Anderson University's campus. He greeted me with a firm handshake and invited me to have a seat. The office was barely big enough for two people since Dr. Froese had arranged floor to ceiling bookshelves in a makeshift serpentine hallway to accommodate his hundreds of books. He guided me to his desk that faced the window overlooking the trees and walking paths below.

After a bit of small talk, he turned toward the letters which he had spread across his desk, put on reading glasses, and bowed his head of white hair like a monk beginning to pray. He opened the first letter, dated 1947 and spoke to me in his thick German accent, "This letter, written by the city priest Heinrich Mohr from the German town of Creglingen, was written just after

WWII, a difficult time for my country. It is a list of your relatives who lived in Baden-Wurttemberg. It looks like your grandmother, Emma Hilpert, had been seeking this genealogical information."

The letter listed the names and life dates of Gottlieb's father, Conrad Dieterich, brother, Johann Christian, and his children and grandchildren, and his sister, Eva Luise (married last name Schule) and her children and grandchildren.

"Oh my, this is incredible!" I said, unable to come up with anything more precise. Emma had the same passion as I; she wanted to know about our family history too!

As Dr. Froese read the next letter, his face turned ashen, and he looked at me with a somber expression. "You know, during and after the war many families were in great distress. In this letter your cousin, Berta Dieterich, is requesting clothing. She stated..." and he read from the letter:

> Concerning clothing, it is very bad and actually impossible to get anything. The consequences of the last war we are getting to experience only now completely. The poor Germans are being driven together into the smallest territory. What will still happen is impossible to foresee. It is very joyous for us that someone from America asks about us in Buchelberg.

I was dumbfounded. Hearing this voice from the past, this voice that had spoken first to my grandmother when she read this very same letter, and now hearing it myself, connected us over time and space. It was exhilarating. Dr. Froese continued.

"Your relatives were highly educated. This letterhead is impressive." He read from Gottlieb Schule, Eva Luise's husband:

> Concerning the contemporary situation in Germany, you must certainly have heard, that after such a long war, a difficult time had to come, for the loser it could not be any other way, that through the bombardments of our cities and factories by the airplanes of the enemies, because of that, the plight of accommodations is terribly great. The creation of the necessary needs for use is far behind the

need. This resulted in an inflation in all areas (a general rise in prices). Our saved pennies have been devalued down to 6 ½ %, in addition to the war debts. We have become a poor people. However this you know yourself and I do not want to extend this sorry chapter any further.

He continued, "Your grandmother was sending items to her first cousins

in Germany. In this letter they are thanking her for sending gifts. This one is from cousin Karl Schule,"

> *Your package has arrived safely. We were very happy about it. We give our best thanks for it. If you would have seen the shining eyes of my children while the package was unpacked you surely would have had tears in your eyes. I would like to especially thank you for the coffee beans, the soap, and strips (yarn).*

Finally, Dr. Froese explained how many families were divided in their political allegiance, some siding with Hitler and some staunchly opposed. He looked at me and said, "Your family was divided in the same way." He picked up a letter in which a cousin revealed his brother Albert was in the Third Reich in a "high position." He put that one down and tapped his finger on a different letter from cousin Karoline, explaining that it revealed that she and her husband were *"very much against Hitler's party."* In fact, her husband was mayor of their town and helped resettle refugees after the war. In addition, their daughter was working with the Red Cross to assist the survivors at the Dachau concentration camp.

He paused, and spoke with weightiness, "These letters are invaluable and speak of the devastation of a war we should never forget. Never."

I nodded. I had nothing to say. I decided at that moment, *yes, I will not forget. I will not forget the victims and survivors of the holocaust. I am ashamed that a member of my own family believed Hitler's lies, his propaganda, his murderous grotesque mission to eradicate the Jewish people.*

Anger about the injustice arose like a geyser, but I rapidly stuffed it down, like applying pressure to an open wound. Not now, this was neither the time nor place.

I slowly placed the letters back in the box and expressed my deep appreciation for the gift Dr. Froese had given — the gift of his time and insights. He bowed his head in humble admiration, thanking me for my research and for keeping the stories alive for generations to come.

Through later research, I learned why Jewish communities throughout Germany were treated as outsiders prior to the holocaust.

> *Jews had suffered periodic expulsion and persecution ever since the Crusades, particularly in the wake of the Black Death peak in the fourteenth century. They were routinely denounced from city and village pulpits as the murderers of Christ. Since most territories and cities denied Jews the rights to own land or to practice most trades and crafts, the majority of them made their living through money lending, trade, and peddling...In this environment, Jewish peddlers with their cheaper goods and their more aggressive approach to sales were deeply resented by the Burger (male citizens) shopkeepers, who expected to wait in their stores for their captive customers. The irony was that the very limitations placed on Jewish ownership of village businesses tended to push them into itinerant, market-oriented practices with which the local businesses could not compete.*[19]

Jewish families in Germany were only allowed to live in specific areas (often called Jewish allies), only allowed to wear certain clothing (sometimes even

[19]Scheer, Teva J. Our Daily Bread: German Village Life, 1500-1850. Adventis Press, 2010.

required to wear a yellow circle), and not allowed to become local citizens with voting rights.

I arrived back at our home — a converted garage that now masqueraded as a three-bedroom house — with a sorrowful expression. Dave asked, "What's wrong? Are you ok? Did everything go ok?"

"It's all too much." I broke down and sobbed, let it flow out; all of it. And then I went to bed.

The next day, I tucked away the letters, the legal pads, the artifacts, the family stories, the curiosities, the heartaches, and the questions. I put them all in a large plastic tub underneath seasonal clothing in a spare closet and closed the door. I promised Dr. Froese I wouldn't forget, but I needed to shift my focus for a season.

Winter came and went, and I started thinking about spring, about getting into the garden again.

part 4: spring

We are who we are because of this land. When we stand upon it, even now, even with all of the changes that have scarred it, marred it, and made it less pure, we can feel the eternal connection that exists for us when our hearts are open[20].
—Richard Wagamese, Walking the Ojibway Path

Every spring I am reminded of God's love for women; when flowers of lavender, pink or yellow bloom with heavenly fragrance.
—Johanna Hilpert

through the gate

After surviving the dark cold months of winter blahs, digging in the dirt anchored me, like roots to a tree. I became sustainable, connected to the earth. Whole again. Seeds were evidence of hope as they sprouted in my yard. This hadn't always been the case. I recalled having a different attitude as an eight-year-old.

———————

On the balls of my feet, I undid the fence latch at the back of the yard. My eyes opened in terror as I stepped into the mysterious and overwhelming space. Light and shadows danced above my head as breezes moved monstrous corn stalks like puppets, warning me to turn back. I looked for my mother, as I carefully walked on a narrow garden path that had been covered with newspaper, trying to avoid the scratchy leaves reaching out to claw at me. I noticed the skin on my arms turning red with itchy bumps, so I tucked my hands into the safety of pant pockets and moved stealthily to the opposite end of the row.

[20]Wagamese, Richard. Walking the Ojibway Path. Milkweed Editions, 2002.

Scanning the garden-scape, I felt overwhelmed, uncomfortable; and my imagination only made it worse. I saw ten-foot vines crawling on the ground like pythons with yellow trumpet blossom heads and stamen tongues. I saw bean vines spiraling up tripod sticks like green smoke from a sinister fire. I heard angry red tomatoes crying out to be freed, held hostage by rusted wire jail cells. Demon bugs taunted as they crept, buzzed, and swooped around my body; I swatted nervously, shooing them with flailing elbows. Finally, I saw Mom near the tree line where she and Mrs. Krist were moving a pile of dead grass clippings, and ran to her side. The caustic smell of decay invaded my nostrils. *This is what death smells like,* I thought, my eight-year-old imagination still powering on. The sun seared my forehead, sweat dripped down my cheeks. I was not fond of being in this strange place; my senses spun out of control. I wanted to leave.

"Mom! MOM! I want to go! It's hot and smelly and scary and I might DIE. Can we please go to the swimming pool? PLEASE!" I moaned.

Mom replied with a sparkle and a smile, "But Julie, look at our beautiful garden! Wouldn't you like to help?"

I almost vomited. "NOOOO! Please!" Even as an eight-year-old I had a flair for the dramatic.

Mrs. Krist turned to me with a look of empathy, wiping sweat off her brow with the back of her arm and offered, "Julie, you are nearly old enough to take care of a garden patch of your own!" I stopped abruptly and gazed up at her with curiosity and confusion.

"My own garden?"

In my 8 years of childhood, I had never cared for a garden space of my own, nor had I wanted to. Gardening was not just an unwelcome inconvenience that required long hours of pulling weeds and getting dirty, but a potentially dangerous experience that could wreak havoc on my sensitive body! But Mrs. Krist said I was old enough, as if she believed I was ready, perhaps responsible, and maybe even courageous enough to become a gardener.

Mr. and Mrs. Krist were faithful friends of my parents. They and their two daughters, Jennifer and Heidi, nearly the same age as my sister and I, lived four blocks south at the edge of the confines of our suburban neighborhood. Their backyard was like ours with plants growing along the fence to soften the edges, but beyond the property line, Mrs. Krist squatted on a field between their house and a busy city street, where she grew a wide variety of vegetables and fruits. Bordered by tall evergreen trees, the 20' x 30' plot was big enough to share, so Mrs. Krist invited my mother, Johanna, to join in the sisterhood of gardening. Mom made regular trips over to the garden during spring and summer months, so she and Mrs. Krist could work side by side.

My own garden, I thought to myself, making a complete 180 from my former disposition. *I'll prove her right!* I turned to Mom and chirped, "Can I, Mom? Can I?"

She laughed, amused by my sudden change of heart. "Yes, but we will have to wait a bit. It's not planting season."

"When will it be planting season?" I asked?

"Next spring, dear." she answered.

"Next spring?"

It seemed like a lifetime away.

———————

Over the winter Mom sat down with me to make a plan. She advised me to grow green beans, tomatoes and lettuce. I requested sunflowers. Though my birth name is Julie, Latin for *youthful one*, "Sunflower" was my chosen name in Indian Maidens. I loved sunflowers. I drew a picture of the future garden on yellow ledger paper Dad had brought home from his accounting job. After lining the paper with rows of plants, I proudly placed it on the refrigerator with a magnet. At the top it read, "Julie's Garden...Coming Soon!"

On a rainy day in April, Mom and I went to the hardware store to purchase the seed packets. I shook them like maracas, dancing and twirling in the aisle. "When can we plant them, Mom? Today? Today?"

She responded with an apologetic smile, "Not till after the last frost. You don't want them to die in a Michigan cold snap."

———————

On our first visit to the garden, Mom explained in her best teacher voice the steps needed to prepare the soil for planting.

"First, let's put on our garden gloves!" She pulled two pairs out of her trug basket, one mom-sized, and a brand-new smaller pair for me. They were checkered pink and fit perfectly. Now I looked the part.

"As we pull out the prickly weeds, the gloves will help protect your hands, since you are prone to getting a rash. Now, watch as I dig down to pull out the entire root. You need to use those arm muscles," she encouraged.

I looked down at my scrawny arms. Would they be strong enough? I was on the swim team, but only a 4th place winner. I tried my best alongside her. "Is this deep enough?" I grunted.

"Nope, deeper still; as deep as your wrist."

Mom demonstrated how to pull out the long root with a gentle rocking motion.

I pulled with impatience, and the top broke off, leaving the root firmly stuck in the ground. This gardening business was hard.

"Mom, when can we plant the seeds?" I huffed.

"Not yet! After pulling the weeds, we need to turn over the soil with a spade shovel and loosen the clumps with a rake. Then we'll add compost to enrich the soil." She looked at me with a loving smile. "You're not giving up already are you?"

I looked down at my knees, dirt-stained and rock-pocked, and sighed. The reality of having a garden began to sink in.

But, Mrs. Krist said I was old enough. So I got back to work.

After preparing the garden bed, Mom showed me how to make neat rows with mounds of soil by tying a string between sticks placed at either end. She taught, "This string will guide you as you plant the seeds. Remember, once a seed goes into the ground, it's like putting it to sleep under a blanket of dirt."

That night, I sank into my own bed sunburned, itchy and exhausted. My imagination got the best of me again as I dreamt of flying above my garden, where giant bugs were destroying the plants.

It was going to be a long summer.

A week later, the day of planting finally arrived. My little sister and I wore brand-new matching blue overalls sewn by Mom, who took our photo.

I skipped back to the garden, undid the latch and took the seeds out of my pocket. "MOM, are you coming?" She took too long talking to Mrs. Krist.

"Mom, did you bring the gloves?"

She arrived momentarily and responded without urgency, "No garden gloves needed this time. You will carefully place two seeds into the palm of your hand, grasp each between your fingers, like so, and plant them about an inch deep, and 4 inches apart. Use this yard stick to space them out properly. Laura, come with me, we can plant marigolds to keep the bugs away!"

I nodded earnestly and was anxious to begin. Spring breezes blew dead leaves into a frenzy, but the morning sun chased cool temperatures away. I shook the seed packets the way Mom had shown and ripped off the top of the envelope. Pouring the smooth oval bean seeds into my hand, I marveled and couldn't imagine how they would become food to eat, or even a plant for that matter. I felt powerful, in charge of this tiny piece of earth. *Two per hole.* I measured, dropped, covered, measured, dropped, covered, over and over and over until the row was complete. The lettuce seeds were miniscule and lifted off my hand with a wisp of air, so I protected them in my fist. I overheard Mom telling Laura how to dig. *I already had that lesson.* I felt so proud.

I kept at it, though my knees ached from squatting. Occasionally, I stood up to stretch out, noticing my armpits felt wet and uncomfortable. With a sigh of resolve, I turned to grab the tomato seedlings, pulled each out of its plastic cell and placed them where I'd dig a hole. Fascinated by the meandering white hairs at the bottom of each plant, I wondered how deep they would grow.

Mom walked over with a wheelbarrow full of compost to check on me. "How is it going, Julie?"

"Good!" I said with confidence.

"The sunflower seeds need to be planted 12 inches apart," Mom reminded.

"I know Mom." I didn't like be told what to do, especially with Laura in the garden.

Again, two per hole, I dropped the black and white sunflower seeds into the earth. I recalled Mrs. Krist saying, "The sunflower is the queen of the garden. She attracts the bees who pollinate our bean, tomato and squash blossoms which, in turn, produce wonderful vegetables and fruit."

I finished by filling the watering can to the brim, requiring both hands to carry and sprinkle water on the seeds and seedlings. I stared intently as if they might pop out of the ground any second. But they didn't. I wanted to sleep in the garden that night, but a fear of bugs convinced me otherwise. Mrs. Krist gave me a few cages to surround the tomato seedlings. I wasn't sure if this would keep danger out, but I hoped it would help.

Before leaving, I asked, "When can we come back?"

Mom chuckled, surprised by my eagerness. "You're funny, Julie Anne! We can come back tomorrow if you like!"

———————

A week later, the lettuce plants shot up side by side, delicate and naked, like paper thin rabbit ears peeking out of a burrow. The bean plants twisted their way up and out of the soil, reaching lime green sepals to the sky. As the sunflowers grew taller with each visit, I measured them against my body: first ankle high, then knee, waist, and eventually they soared above my head. Dad came once to check on the progress of my garden. He lifted me in his arms so I might look at the sunflowers eye to eye. I could swear they smiled and winked at me, saying, "Hello, Sunflower!"

We made countless trips to the garden that summer. I worked alongside my mentors, watching and listening. It was a rite of passage. Mrs. Krist and Mom taught me how to watch for and protect plants from pests, like the slimy grubs that made holes in the lettuce. They kept out rabbits with baffling powdered dried blood. They taught me that when two green bean seeds sprout side by side, only one can thrive, so you have to pick out the weaker plant. They taught me when to pick the ripened tomatoes and how to snap a green bean off the stem. Mom suggested I eat the freshly picked green beans, without washing them first! Beans never tasted so good, crunchy and surprisingly sweet. The sunflower queens grew at least 8 feet tall, and the worker bees came and went, humming their songs of productivity. I worked harder than I'd ever worked before, and I was happy and felt accomplished, having endured the rigor of gardening.

Like a child off to school, I strapped these formative experiences on my back, not realizing their significance and how they'd given me an instruction manual for resilience. I had purpose, tending to the plants that needed me. I was gratified to harvest plants for the family dinner table. The gate, no longer an entrance to a scary unknown world, was a passage to life; the invitation to steward a piece of that world rooted me in a warm, crumbly, moist soil, where I blossomed.

As autumn approached, the plants eventually turned brown and withered. On one of our last visits before starting fourth grade I asked my garden mentors, "Am I a real gardener now?" Mrs. Krist and my mother looked at me approvingly and nodded.

I was one of the sisters of the garden.

Julie in her garden

Johanna, Gary, Julie and Laura at Grandma Emma's garden

back in time

I began writing at the age of 11, after purchasing a yellow flower-patterned journal at the corner pharmacy. The empty lines had endless possibilities for my evolving creativity. I wrote plays, enacting them with a neighborhood friend on her back deck, a make-shift stage. Princess costumes were created out of old sheer curtains, and dragons made with camp stools. The audience consisted of my friend's mother, sister and brothers.

During eighth grade my teacher told me I had talent, after reading a writing assignment in which I described the amazement of chocolate cake. I began experimenting with writing songs and poetry; words penned on the page illuminated pictures in my mind. Emboldened by my teacher's praise, I wrote to a publishing company asking for the submission packet. I had found an ad in the back of a magazine suggesting I could become an author. Recalling a scene from *Little Women* in which Jo packaged her manuscript to send off to the publisher, I was intent on doing the same. The company, however, wanted lots of money up front, so my author's dreams were dashed before they'd really had a chance to take off.

Looking back, I think there was something prescient about my experience with that publishing company. I had found comfort and identity in writing. My creative mind was generating ideas to share with the world. But when I opened that manila-colored envelope and read that the company wanted something from me before I could really share my voice, I think I internalized that the world probably didn't want my ideas anyway. The world didn't need my voice.

By 15, my journal became a place to express swirling emotions. I wrestled with melancholy boyfriend woes, and a growing ache to belong. Insecurity became a daily companion, as did heavy make-up and punk-rock music. I experimented with cigarettes and alcohol. I worked at fitting in; at pleasing others as a way of finding myself. My boyfriend, the focal point of so many of my attempts to find myself, gave me the attention I craved. I trusted him, and my innocence became an *in* for his predation. I lost my voice and he took my virginity.

On January 28, 1986, the Space Shuttle Challenger exploded, an expedition gone terribly wrong, and somehow I could relate. Life had spun out of control. I worried that I was pregnant. I stopped writing. I stopped caring. Stuck in a cycle of back-and-forth relationship games. I became the undignified loser. I gave myself over to unhealthy coping mechanisms, and one that would stay with me for decades: pulling out eyelashes.

At 17, I started attending Wayne State University in Detroit on a dance scholarship. Throughout my childhood, involvement in theater and dance provided an outlet for creative expression as well as a path toward physical and emotional well-being. I enjoyed the camaraderie of a dance production, the hard work of learning and executing complex choreography, and expressing outwardly an inner concept. In dance classes at Wayne, I found more than classmates, as early in that first semester I became acquainted with Darci, Marci and Christine. We became a fast foursome in and out of class.

But at the end of our freshman year, life changed overnight for Darci. Diagnosed with an aggressive cancerous brain tumor, she was given months to live. Soon her long auburn hair had fallen out and was replaced with bandanas to protect her scalp. Her once fluid movements became stilted and unsteady. I couldn't understand why or how this could happen to such a vibrant and beautiful 18-year-old.

At the time, my professor of Shakespearean Literature required us to keep a journal to freely express our thoughts and feelings as we read plays and poems. I became acquainted with the characters, identifying with their grief, their conflicts, their mental anguish. I became friends with Ophelia, a young woman ordered around by men who would talk about her, not to her. "We know what we are, but know not what we may be," Shakespeare wrote in *Hamlet*.[21] The professor had given me permission to wrestle, to question, to seek and respond however I felt compelled.

As Darci's health declined we stuck by her side, visiting her at her parents' home when we could. We would sit in the living room together, singing, crying, and holding hands even on the darkest days, when she was too weak to get out of bed. Her mother Gayle would often tearfully embrace us in the entry way as we were leaving and express appreciation for our faithfulness. Togetherness, this loyalty to our sisterhood, gave Darci some comfort, and provided me, Christine, and Marci the strength to deal with the pain of our

---

[21]Shakespeare, William. 1564-1616 author. The Tragedy of Hamlet, Prince of Denmark.
[London] :The Folio Society, 1954.

collective broken dreams. Through it all, Darci modeled contentment despite her devastating debilitating circumstances. She often spoke about faith and hope, never complaining, and smiling like an angel. Because of Darci, the three of us had the strength to sing at her funeral.

In the spring of that freshman year, Christine invited me to join a Christian fellowship group on campus. I wasn't sure if I was particularly interested in a bunch of churchy college students, but I was attracted to Christine's sincerity, so after putting her off for several months, I realized maybe being around some sincere, kind people would be a welcome change. She invited me to attend a weekend retreat, and I agreed. My goal: meeting a nice guy. I needed to find a man who might treat me better.

After an hour's drive out to the small town near the camp, and an additional drive along a meandering twisting seasonal gravel road, we arrived at Pinewood. As I carried my backpack to the dormitory from the car, I noticed a figure in a blue and green rugby shirt standing at the top of a hill under the overhead camp-light, where moths and bugs were basking. He was standing with friends laughing, joking.

It was Dave.

I approached the group to say hello, ostensibly to everyone, but I really wanted to see Dave again, to see if he remembered me. We had met briefly only a couple of weeks prior, and there was something about him that I just, well. I was attracted to his gregarious smile and warm brown eyes. Other than the rugby shirt, he was in khakis rolled and pinned at the ankle, and a pair of Sperry Topsider shoes. Dave was taller than me by 4 inches, with a fit physique narrowing to a trim waist; he had a runner's body.

It didn't take long for me to laugh at his jokes. It's not that all of them were funny; it's just that there were so many of them! He began to win me over on the sheer volume of his jokes and light-heartedness. My stomach ached from so much laughter. It was a release, a *relief*, a redemptive beginning. I tucked my name and phone number in his shirt pocket the day we packed up to leave.

During the retreat, the speaker prompted me to consider faith in Creator, intelligent and infinitely loving; in Jesus, redemptive healer, who delights in our beauty; and in Spirit, comforter, giver of strength. A profound spiritual reversal took place in my mind and heart. I even felt it in my body. As I sat alone on a stone step overlooking the forest, layers of shame dissolved into the ground; I emerged feeling lighter, freer.

Not long after that weekend, Dave and I started dating. While I enjoyed his company, Dave seemed almost too perfect. I'd never known someone like him. Especially a boy. But in time we grew to trust each other through vulnerable conversations. I shared honestly about my scars from the past; Dave listened without judgement. He wooed me with kindness and affirmation. In a poem Dave compared me to a pure white rose. I felt profoundly beautiful, and deeply grateful.

Something was growing in me. I started writing again: love letters to God; love letters to Dave. The two of us spent four years dating and discovering our shared love of nature, of music, of art, of literature. And we shared a deep love for northern Michigan, visiting his family's cottage on Burt Lake as often as we could.

So it was both a surprise and welcome culmination when on a perfect Saturday evening in May, Dave came to the house where I rented a room, to initiate an evening of romance. He began by presenting me with a dozen red roses, and took us to a new locale where he gave me the first in a series of thoughtful poems and meaningful gifts. Each led to an enchanted moment when we stood under the shelter of a white gazebo in the center of a quiet historic street as a small jazz ensemble played nearby. He knelt as a gentleman and asked for my hand in marriage.

I said yes, kissing him as tears streamed down my face.

Dave and I married the following spring on May 23rd, when lilacs bloomed, filling the air with sweet well-wishes. I felt beloved, like a worthy sunflower queen on our wedding day and we consummated our love, having waited for this commemorative day.

A year later, after graduating from Wayne State, we moved away from home for the first time in our lives, to begin a new chapter in Indiana, where Dave would attend seminary at Anderson University and I would begin my career as a teacher.

Life was both exciting and challenging during that time, and as we were trying to create our new life in a new state, I rarely had time to write. After a couple years, I settled into the new reality and felt my voice growing in strength. Like I was ready to write once again. So when I saw an advertisement for a local writing class, I signed up. I thought it would provide a place to be inspired, learning from other writers.

The leader proposed we reflect on personal pain and how we were, or would someday, deal with loss. She recommended we read a book about grieving by Walter Wangerin Jr. and quoted, *"Death doesn't wait till the ends of our lives to meet us and to make an end, instead, we die a hundred times before we die, and all the little endings on the way are like a slowly growing echo of the final BANG! Yet out of our many losses, our 'little deaths,' comes a truer recognition of life."* But this was not the kind of inspiration I had in mind. I was dismissive. And sorely disappointed.

The rest of the women in the group were in their 40s or 50s, but as a 26-year-old, I was not ready to dig deep into the ways I'd experienced pain or loss, and I was certainly not willing to write openly about these experiences. In fact, I was afraid to think about dying; I didn't want to be like my friend Darci who died so young. I wrote a half-honest piece, and stopped going.

Dave graduated from Anderson University and began his career as a pastor in Indianapolis, where I too found a job working in the same church with the children's ministry.

It was time to settle in to our adult lives, so we purchased our first house, a 1920's one-story bungalow with high ceilings, transom windows and wood floors. And in front of the house, were sidewalks. A house with sidewalks, was the perfect place to start a family. The time seemed right for Dave and I to begin discussions about the possibility of having children. Getting pregnant was harder than we expected, but on December 21, 1996, Noah, whose Hebrew name means both *rest* and *motion,* the latter being more applicable, was born. A few years later, after a scare with preterm labor and 7 weeks of strict bedrest, Nathanael, whose Hebrew name means *gift of God,* was born on September 14, 2000.

Our family became a budding grove of trees.

side walks

little boys

Under my arm
Facing outward
They ran on air
And then on two feet
And they haven't stopped since
Running, splashing, throwing
In constant motion.

Slow down, look, there's a garden snake slithering away on the trail.
Stop, let's paint the leopard frog peeking out from the pond.
Turn around, look, a raccoon is hobbling through the forest.

They listened
Slowed down
And stopped,
But only for a second.

I chased them on sidewalks
Through dandelion fields
Up to painted clouds
Across stoney beaches
Under fresh water waves
Over slatted bridges
And into dozens of forests
Where forts became
Home
For a minute.

Then one day they stopped
To watch Father sun set upon the water
And Mother moon rise at night.
You said, listen, there's a barred owl hooting.
You said, wake up, there's a morning dove making a nest.
You said, let's go there's a new trail to explore.

And I turned to look
But they had gone.

Little boys don't last forever,
But I was changed, forever.

to dad's workshop

Mom and Dad regularly visited Indianapolis to spend time with their growing grandsons. One year at Christmas, when the boys were ages 6 and 2, Mom and Dad came with a car full of presents. Dad, who our kids called Grandpa Gary, loved playing with his grandsons. He took them for rides on his shoulders around the house. They watched videos of trains and built elaborate Thomas the Tank Engine sets. But this time Dad seemed off. We noticed he was spilling coffee more than normal, complained of a constant headache, and was unable to remember circumstances and directions. He got lost going to Walmart to buy us a broom. This was unusual. Dad had always been competent with directions.

After returning home to Lathrup Village, Dad visited the doctor, and through a series of tests, he received a terminal diagnosis: Glioblastoma; a cancerous brain tumor, incurable and inoperable. They gave him three months to live. He was 63.

Every night I went to bed hoping to wake up and realize it was just a bad dream. But it wasn't. How could this be possible?

A few years prior, Laura and her husband Jon had moved to Indianapolis for work. Jon had been searching for a job throughout the U.S. and landed at a job in Fishers, only 10 miles from where Dave and I lived. Their proximity was a huge blessing, as we were able to get together regularly, especially once Laura gave birth to Evan, whose Welsh name means *God is Gracious*. We raised our sons together, rooting them in similar values.

So it was a comfort to be able to support one another during Dad's illness. After the diagnosis, Laura and I returned home to Lathrup together. We were united in our emotional suffering, in the disbelief, in the anger. Our sisterhood saved us.

Hurled into intense care for Dad, Mom had no choice but to make the best of every day. She had faith like a rock. Laura and I tried to follow Mom's example of faith, singing lyrics by Matt Redman, "When the darkness closes in, Lord, still I will say, blessed be the name of the Lord."[22] We counted on healing. And we felt like we were getting it, albeit in small doses.

---

[22]Redman, Matt. Blessed Be Your Name: The Songs of Matt Redman Vol. 1. Survivor Records. UK, 2005.

Dad didn't die in three months like the doctors predicted. He lingered, but that lingering provided time with him that was invaluable. No longer able to run off and complete chores around the house, or tune ups on the car, or tweaks to his model train exhibit, he had to be present. In the same room. No more excuses.

On one visit, Dad asked if I could take him to an evening gathering with his train buddies. I was happy to go, but wondered how grown men *played trains*. This was a pastime Dad had enjoyed for as long as I could remember. It was a boys' club — no girls allowed. But the circumstances had changed, and Dad invited me to accompany him. I was not about to say no.

Welcomed by Ron, Dad's old friend and the leader of the event, we were directed to the basement where the action was already taking place. I helped Dad carefully descend the stairs; his coordination now perceptibly waning. Once we'd reached the basement floor I glanced over at a group of about 12 men intensely focused on the operation of a massive train set sprawling from one end of the basement to the other. Each participant had a role to play and a job to do, each delineated on a piece of paper.

I watched as Dad tried his best to join the action, his cheeks puffy from steroids, and his eyes slow to move. One by one, as Dad shuffled around the room, men stopped to greet him, helping him to feel a part of the camaraderie, ignoring the apparent changes in Dad's body, and avoiding the word "cancer."

All those years that Dad hid himself in a basement corner constructing and painting the various elements of a miniature village, I didn't get it. He could disappear for hours to hunch over his workbench pouring his energies into a replica storefront, and foregoing time spent with me, with us. I was impressed by his skilled handiwork, and I was proud of his ability to create, but as I grew up, his choices angered me, puzzled me. Ultimately, I unintentionally internalized a message: I wasn't worthy of the attention. So, if attention wasn't going to be given, I would seek it and take it where I could.

Occasionally, I would visit Dad in his workshop. But you had to be invited. It was not a world you wandered into on your own. So, when he would invite me to enter his sacred space, I would always take him up on the offer. He would show me the process of taking a model kit — a storefront or a Victorian home — and to make it look like a believable miniature artifact for his exhibit. He hoped to have the train group visit his basement one day, to play trains. That day never came.

Mom worked all day as a teacher, and nursed Dad all night. To say it was exhausting would be a vast understatement. Sometimes her smile faded after those long days, but she rarely let us or anyone see the toll it was all taking. Eventually Dad was unable to ascend the stairs, so a hospital bed was installed in the dining room, where he could listen to jazz 24-7 on the old stereo. Lying in that bed, listening to the music that stirred him in deep and mysterious ways, he would often be brought to tears. Cleansing tears. And when he couldn't sleep, the anxieties enveloping him, Mom would brew some hot chocolate and sit with him, hold his swollen hands and assuage his fears about the unassessed roof repairs, the unfinished train village, or the long-promised but never-started renovation of the master bedroom.

That October — over ten months since his diagnosis, and a full seven months longer than he was expected to live — the entire family went on a weekend getaway to Frankenmuth, Michigan. Dad smiled proudly as he watched his grandsons swimming in the hotel pool, taking photos of them from his wheelchair. He graciously insisted that he and Mom pay for our hotel stay and the delicious chicken dinner at Zehnder's Restaurant. Our time together was irreplaceable and, we knew, unrepeatable.

Upon our return, Dad's condition declined precipitously.

Writing became my salve. Journaling enabled me to express profound grief. I remembered the women in the writing class I'd visited a decade earlier, and the leader's encouragement to write about loss. I didn't want to then. I had no choice now. I needed to accept the unfathomable. I was losing my daddy.

Fear and faith fought like enemies in my brain. I hated both, and neither made sense. But I remembered Aunt Martha, Emma, and Amelia who had lost both parents and leaned on each other, throughout the hardships. Their survival story gave me strength. Hope.

My writing took on a new form, too, as I began to write Dad's words down. He dropped quotes like packages at my front door and on every visit. I recorded this love pouring from his heart to ours. They say, the dying offer gifts. My dying father gave pearls of wisdom. All the anger and unforgiveness

I had carried toward him for the unhealthy ways he had communicated or completely missed the mark as a *present* father melted away. I found courage to say, "I forgive you, Dad." To this he replied, "I'm sorry, Julie," and shared vulnerably the ways in which he was mistreated by his own father. Secrets revealed. Secrets I understood.

While his deteriorating condition was saddening, his growing peace and submission to his end-of-life diagnosis was inspiring. "I'm going on ahead to check out the new territory," he once said, considering his impending death. "God is in charge. He knows my mind and heart. My life is in His hands. Whatever he sees for my future is what will be. Whatever the outcome, I'll accept his fate for me. I'm not asking for a miracle. All you can do is live one day at a time and try to keep your heart right. It's a lifelong process—figuring out who's in charge. I feel confident. He's been good to me."

And he helped bring healing to me by articulating his regret on the one hand, and his pride on the other. "If I could do my life over, I'd be more devoted to Jesus' saving grace. He gives us the peace that passes all understanding. And I'd have been a more attentive father and husband. I'm so blessed to have a family—I'm proud of how you use your gifts for God. You guys are the best thing that's happened to me. I wish I could love you more; I'll love you forever."

Dad taught me how to live, and how to die. His life came to an end on January 27, 2004, on Mom's birthday. He was 64, just like his grandfather Gottlieb.

After Dad was gone, instead of pearls of wisdom, depression and anxiety dropped off packages at my front door. I opened them and carried them everywhere. I couldn't cry; I was stuck in a spiral moving downward, grappling with unresolved questions about Dad's life, about our relationship, or absence of one. The healing I experienced through his dying season was real, but that was between us. Now I had to reckon with *myself.* But my story was inextricably linked to Dad's and I desperately wanted to understand the story behind his pain.

I found myself in the basement of my childhood home wandering into Dad's workshop looking for answers. I focused on the small bottles of paint, a myriad of colors, lined up neatly on a hand-made shelf above the workbench. *Dad was an artist,* I thought. This I understood.

side walks

the artist

part 1

Sorry, you're not cut out for college
Your grades aren't up to par
They told him
Before diagnoses of
ADHD and Dyslexia were answers
Before IEP's and 504's were offered
Before OCD and depression were treated
He was labeled as incapable, lazy, dumb.
The factory welcomed him in
Exposing his young creative mind to toxins
Wasting his brain potential on
Industrial sludge.
But I can play the trumpet
Jazzy like Louis A
Cool like Miles D!
Son, I've had to work hard
To support a family. You can't
Raise a family as a musician!
But I'm good with my hands
I can put together a model car
Forwards and back
Without reading the instructions.
I can visualize.
Seems like you are a concrete thinker
What about accounting?

side walks

part 2

The artist worked
With numbers during the day
But with paints at night
His hands and eyes in a
Symbiotic relationship
Creating a three dimensional
Utopia, miniature yet real
An escape.
The cold concrete block studio
In the farthest corner of the
Basement next to the screeching
Monstrous furnace, was a
Refuge for his weary
Brain, tired from numbers
And people
And corporate games.
Colonial colors in glass jars
Lined up side by side
Contained a touch of Williamsburg class.
Each train-station
Each hardware-store
Each stately home
Each train car
Was painted to look weathered-old
Beautiful
Authenticity the goal.
With paint brushes, hairs as delicate as
Eyelashes, he painted using painful
Accuracy
Slipping out an occasional Son of a Bitch
When something wasn't just right.
With each tree,
Each track
Each representative element
He moved closer and closer to the big
Reveal
The reenactment
The night when friends would
Gather in the studio to
Marvel at his
Handiwork.

side walks

part 3

I'm sorry, but these headaches
You're experiencing are not normal
The x-rays show
An inoperable brain tumor
Could be related to
Chemical exposure.
Have you ever worked in a
Factory?
Glioblastoma.
The artist painted as long as he could
Descend the stairs
To the studio.
He visited friend's
Studios
Applauded their work.
His collected dust.
He recalled the corporation.
They said, if you don't quit
We'll make it hell for you
To work here.
So he quit
Spending years trying to find
A new job
As a 50-year-old man, he
Settled on the sale of stocks
And handyman jobs.
Depression set in.
Value diminished.
He finally decided to
See a doctor and was
Prescribed an SSRI.
A few months later
He was diagnosed with
Incurable cancer.

side walks

part 4

After the artist died
It was all sold.
There is one creation
Left.
A house.
One.

Memories are still strong
And the time spent
With the artist
Time watching
His large steady hands
Paint while calling
Attention to details I would have
Missed
Time listening to his
Strong breath
In and out
Chest slowly rising
And falling
Under a soft blue sweatshirt
Indicating the level of focus
Peace
Escape
Time observing the pursuit of a
Dream
A grand vision.
Time spent
With the artist
Gives some closure.

And I wonder if it wasn't the
Art that mattered
But the
Act
Of making the Art
In a community with
Other artists
Who understood
The Beauty
Of it all

into hiding

As a young widow living on her own 300 miles from me and Laura, Mom carried on. Persevered. But there was also a sense of relief, I think. Release. She was finally free to make her own decisions. She loved Dad deeply, but now she would learn to live life on her terms. She grew in confidence and the ability to re-write the trajectory of her next chapter. With the help of Dave and Jon, they cleaned out six dumpsters of "stuff" compulsive Dad had collected and stored in every possible alcove in my childhood home, including a garage attic jammed from floor to ceiling with wood Dad had rescued from trash for his "projects."

Soon after, Mom moved to suburban Indianapolis, into her dream house, not too far from where Laura and I lived. She became actively involved in our lives and the lives of her three grandchildren, cementing our family together in ways we'd not experienced since moving away. I had no idea how crucial this would be for my ability to survive the days to come.

Four years and one month after Dad died, lightning struck on a blue-sky kind of day, and my marriage of 16 years burned, nearly completely to the ground.

I was gone for the weekend, spending time with the boys at a friend's home in Michigan, and returned to find candles had been lit in our home. It was odd. I was suspicious. I searched my mind for some reasonable explanation, and the only conclusion I could draw was the one I was most afraid of. After a series of desperate questions, Dave admitted to having an affair.

My life blew up, broke apart, and scattered like broken egg shells brutally tossed out of a raided nest. I stood in the middle of that nest, rejected, dizzy, lost, and completely alone; without a husband, without a dad.

My heart was singed; an unrecognizable persistent pain settled into every movement, every breath. My body moved, but my mind was absent, in shock, pale face, body wasting, unable to eat, to sleep. "Change the locks." I was advised.

A week after the incomprehensible revelation, tears stopped flowing; sadness became rage. I didn't know the man I had married, it felt like he was completely gone. I changed the locks. I insisted we meet with a lawyer to start the process of a legal separation. That day I returned home, to a place I no longer felt safe, and fell to the kitchen floor. It was cool, vinyl on concrete, solid, immovable, and eased the burn. After laying there for unknown hours, like a drunk woman passed out, I felt Creator say, "Get up," and sun rays peered in through a window, lifting my eyes from the charred remains. A song voiced; *it feels like it might be hope.*[23]

Earlier in our marriage, before kids and career and stress, Dave and I had driven through the State of Washington, through an area destroyed by fire. The smell permeated my nostrils, my hair, my clothes, and prevented my ability to breathe with ease. The blackness was inescapable. Ugliness everywhere. I asked Dave to drive out of the area as fast as possible. I craved green, even a blade of grass would do. The blue sky appeared as dark and hopeless as the earth below.

But there is a marvelous seed; *Wild Hollyhock.* It cracks and germinates *only in extreme heat during a forest fire.* When the fire has been extinguished, and the rains have begun, the seeds absorb water and sprout. All other vegetation has been destroyed. These brave flowers cover the ash, the destruction, the hopelessness with green and pale pink beauty. Nothing is more lovely. Resilience.

Once Peter, a disciple of Jesus, asked how many times we shall forgive one who wrongs us, "Seven times?" Jesus responded, "Seventy-seven times."

I called a friend, and asked her to recommend a counselor who had dealt with experiences like ours: with couples involved in church ministry whose marriage had crashed and burned. When I called Dan Crosley at White River Christian Church's Counseling Center, he said, "Yes, I have counseled couples in your situation; let's meet."

Dan was a guide through the loss. As an older man, former missionary, and quiet listener, he helped me feel safe sorting through layers of confusion. Sometimes I just looked at the floor trying to disentangle thoughts, saying nothing. Sometimes he asked questions that prompted tears I couldn't stop. And sometimes he offered wise words that I furiously wrote in a small journal; words that just might help me stay afloat.

Months of individual counseling opened a door to intense joint sessions

[23]Groves, Sara. It Might Be Hope. Album: Tell Me What You Know. INO Records, 2007.

with Dan. There Dave and I sat, side by side for the first time in three months, to see if there were any seeds in the charred earth. I was scared. I knew something had been wrong, but had no idea how wrong. As we sat there together, I asked if our marriage was salvageable. Dan said yes; that there was a way to reconcile and recreate a strong bond, but it would require hard work. And courage.

Dave had begun to show me that he was not a monster; I saw a glimpse that maybe we could redeem what had been lost. Because I trusted Dan, I was open to his counsel about strategies to facilitate reconnection. He suggested Dave and I meet at a neutral spot to begin to get reacquainted. Face to face. He suggested we start with a conversation about our 2nd grade teacher. We met at the local library on the second floor near a bank of windows and awkwardly started a conversation that would begin to open us up to one another again, creating new roots.

But rebuilding our marriage required more than an emotional bond. We had to make a living. At the time I was a freelance choreographer without work, and Dave had lost his job. He found a very part-time position greeting guests at a local museum and a full-time job as a telemarketer working nights. It was a step. But I still battled the disorientation of being alone. The insecurities and self-doubt that accompany betrayal.

I couldn't have survived without the support and nurturing female presence of my mother and sister, who came at a moment's notice, who would sit with me and cry, and pray, and hold my arms up on the weakest days. And of friends who stuck by my side, without judgement. During this season, the boys stayed with me in our home, and Dave lived with friends who generously offered him a room.

TJ Maxx to the rescue. Shopping always helps! I decided to take off my wedding rings, and replace them with a ring representing my connection to God. TJ Maxx has great jewelry, and cheap. So I found a trio of silver rings with a blue stone, and wore it as a reminder of a scripture, "For I am the Lord your God, who takes hold of your right hand, and says to you, Do not fear; I will help you." Isaiah 41:13. This was a deliberate step of trust. I also prayed like mad. One night when I was distraught and crying out to a God I didn't believe in, I asked for a sign. As I was laying in my bed, alone, I felt the bed shaking. I jolted out of bed as if holy God was in my midst and got on my knees. The shaking continued. I voiced, "OK God, I believe!" The next morning I found out there had been a rare midwestern earthquake.

A turning point came when Dan shared a parable of forgiveness in an individual counseling session with me. In the story a character chose to set down the rocks of bitterness and unforgiveness he'd been carrying, since they were of no help to him on his journey. While Dave and I had been taking steps toward reconciliation, no decisions had been made. I didn't know if I could trust him again. I didn't know if I could forgive — really forgive — and build a life together. But after Dan Crosley read me that parable, something stirred inside me. Spirit awakened in me the vision of an alternate ending to our story. I could offer forgiveness to Dave, because I, too, was in need of forgiveness.

That night I wrote two letters to Dave.

After our next counseling session together, right before he had to drive downtown to his telemarketing job, I said, "Come sit in my car. I have something I want you to read." Dave slid into the passenger seat of my burgundy Subaru Outback, and looked at me curiously. I reached into a folder and handed him two pieces of paper. On top was letter #1, in which I spewed all the anger and disappointment I embodied regarding the affair and how it destroyed me and our relationship. I held nothing back. It was angry. It was harsh. It was true. He read it aloud.

At the end of the letter, however, under my signature, I had written a final message: *Please destroy this letter.*

Dave looked at me quizzically. I smiled and nodded. "Go ahead." He wadded the letter up and threw it at his feet. Then he saw that there was a second letter.

In letter #2, I admitted my own failures, my humanity, and the realization that any and all humans are capable of destruction. I wrote, *I love you and am in love with you.* I told him I forgave him and I asked him for his forgiveness. I shared that I realized I had been an absent partner, like my father. Through tears welling in his eyes, he said, "Of course. Of course I forgive you."

At the end of the letter, under my signature, I added a final message: *Please save this letter.*

Dave and I worked hard to reconcile; harder than we'd ever worked at the notion of relationship, of respect, of loving beyond self. Eighteen weeks from the day our marriage shattered, we rededicated ourselves to our marriage, before friends, family, and — most importantly — before our sons. We made new promises to one another and to them. It was a new beginning, for sure, but it took over two years of walking with intention through the stench of destruction to be able to turn back and see the forest floor covered in green with breakthrough pockets of pale pink hollyhocks. Vulnerability and honesty about loneliness, conversations about emotional distancing, distractions, and anger composted into fertile soil.

In my journal I wrote: *Perhaps it is only through the pain of loss and loneliness that we as humans lower ourselves to meet the soil, breath its stories, eat its nutrients, and dig deeply, until we find resolve, grit, roots that remind us to plant more seeds, so new trees will miraculously grow from these dark places, proving to us that hope is possible, and a forest can be restored. Fire has power to refine, to purify, to provide a fresh start.*

Friends have asked, "How did you survive?" It took two people. Two messed up people. Two messed up people willing to submit to the decades long process of uncovering layers of unhealthy coping mechanisms and mistrust. Pages and pages of journaling. Hours and hours of counseling, both individual and together. Meeting with friends who have survived. Meeting with friends who believed redemption was possible. And time. Time away from each other. And time to reconnect and rebuild. Why? Because we chose to join God in writing a story of beauty from ashes.

to uncle arnold's home

The loss and reconnection Dave and I had endured was like a long winter followed by a slow spring thaw. There were rainy days and windy nights, but the sun had started to shine a bit brighter and warmer, and I had begun to see the blooms of a new relationship pushing up through the earth. During that season my attention had been wholly on the *present* and how we might build a preferred future. But once our spring had really taken hold, it felt like I could breathe again.

We were both ready for a transition of some sort, and decided a good next step would be to move away from the suburban neighborhood in which we'd lived, and into the city. This was a time of envisioning and re-making, and it felt like a fresh start for the next chapter of our life together. We found a 2-bedroom craftsman style home on a leafy street in a neighborhood called Broad Ripple, close to a bicycle and walking trail, restaurants and shops.

As I was packing up a closet while preparing to move, I found the plastic tub with all the family artifacts I'd collected years ago. Opening the lid reminded me of the musty smell of Aunt Martha's old trunk. I thoughtfully reacquainted myself with the stories of life and loss by reading the interviews, the research, the documents and letters I had so zealously collected. I was struck by how I'd changed. When first encountering the pain of the Dieterich family, I couldn't fathom experiencing such heartache, but as a woman who had walked through my own heartache, I could identify with their gratitude for survival.

Aunt Martha lived to be 99 years old. She spent the last of her days in a nursing home, where for once in her life she was the recipient of care, rather than the caregiver. I had been able to introduce her to our infant firstborn son, Noah, a couple of years before. She bounced him on her knee with all the strength she could muster, shining with admiration. We received a gift of money from her estate that helped us pay for the hospital bills during my bed rest for our second-born, Nathanael, who was born on her birthday. Even in her death, she was taking care of us.

Aunt Mitzy lived to be 81 years old. After her husband Fred passed from cancer, she lived as a widow; but since she was childless, my parents took good care of her during that lonely season. My last visit with Aunt Mitzy was the day she gave me her typewritten story.

The storytellers, the matriarchs, had "gone on to the new territory" as Dad said. As I sorted through the various pieces of the Dieterich narrative, I recognized someone had to become the protector of the story, or it would be lost in the generation to come. I felt like I was the next "sister" to prepare the soil, to sow the seeds, to write the story for the next generation. And though I was no longer able to mine information from my great aunts and my father, there was one storyteller who lived on: my dad's older brother, Uncle Arnold.

Arnold resided in Florida with his wife Gloria. After Dad's passing, I felt comforted whenever I could chat with Uncle Arnie who sounded just like Dad. The deep timbre, easy laughter, and slow reflectiveness were all so familiar. Uncle Arnold and I had much in common and enjoyed easy conversations about classical music, walks in nature, spirituality, reading books on social issues, and reminiscing about our family history. As I embraced my sense of calling to shepherd the Dieterich history, I knew that Uncle Arnie was my next partner.

summer at the dieterich farm
(written by arnold hilpert)

I am the 87-year-old son of my deceased mother Emma Marie Dieterich Hilpert. I will be forever grateful that she had me stay on the family farm of her origins in Brutus, Michigan. I have memories of two summers in the mid 1940's when I stayed for about six weeks as a preteen lad — allegedly to 'help out'. I know my 'help' was minimal — especially at pulling weeds in a substantial produce garden. I did, however, learn about life on a subsistence family farm with its many chores and daily rhythms.

Awakening at dawn to the tinkle of cowbells, I would look out the attic bedroom screen and see deer grazing in the cow pasture. My uncle Carl taught me to milk a cow — the old-fashioned way. The field cat, with one eye missing, would always show up for his share at a very crusty bowl. The milking ritual occurred each morning and early evening followed by the humming of the 'separator' in the working kitchen. The 'skim milk' would be taken to the hog's pen where they would squeal with delight at the sight. The dairy cream would be poured into large galvanized containers and set on the porch each morning for the dairy pickup.

Breakfast was 'substantial.' Aunt Martha still used a wood burning stove. Water came from a pump house a few yards from the house. It was carried in a large white pail, discolored from iron in the water, and kept conveniently in the kitchen for drinking with a dipper, cooking, and personal washing. Other hygiene involved the basic outhouse with three different sized holes for diverse family bottoms. The only bath I recall was in a large cast iron tub used for scalding hogs after slaughter. It was filled with water to warm in the sun until I could be convinced to get clean.

Eggs had to be brought in from the chicken coop, but I never mastered the high-risk skill of reaching under a sitting hen. There was a large movable tree stump in the back yard that was stained with the blood of many chicken beheadings. That is where I witnessed that a chicken really can run with its head cut off. Grotesque!

On Saturdays, Aunt Martha would load up the '34 Ford bustle back sedan with eggs and produce for her regular customers. Her route would end in Petoskey, a visit with a relative and friends, and an ice cream cone.

Sunday involved worship at a simple frame Evangelical and Reformed Church. Women sat one side — men on the other. Across the road was their cemetery where my mother's parents and several siblings are buried.

I cherish these memories of a family that lived off the land with hard work and dignity.

———————

Uncle Arnold and Aunt Gloria invited me and Dave to visit their home in the Jacksonville, Florida area which we did one cold March. In their historic retirement community of Penney Farms, founded by J.C. Penney for his parents, there was a beautiful pond with a walking trail surrounding it. One evening on an after-dinner stroll, we stopped at a gazebo with twin swings facing each other. Dave sat next to Gloria, and I sat next to Arnold. He put a fatherly arm around my shoulders like the bough of an elder pine. He had little idea how meaningful this small gesture was to me. It was a palpable love that healed. We sat and rocked for several minutes. I would have been content to stay for hours.

Back at their home, Uncle Arnold and Aunt Gloria shared openly about their lives. Gloria talked about the difficulties of living in the U.S. as a German immigrant family during and after WWII. Arnold spoke about his activism in the Civil Rights movement in Chicago and his work to integrate a racially diverse community as pastor of a Lutheran church. Gloria spoke as a mother does about her sons and grandchildren. "You know, Mark found peace and joy

"Blood and Fire" (self portrait) Mark Hilpert

in an accepting community in the Vineyard Church," she said, referring to her younger son.

For years I had been deeply curious how Arnold and Gloria maintained their own joy and peace and faith when their son Mark died of paranoid schizophrenia; like Aunt Kathleen. I'd always been reticent to bring it up, not wanting to open old wounds, not wanting to be a burden. But in their presence I realized that Mark was not a problem to be avoided. He was a son to be remembered. So I asked. Uncle Arnold invited me to look through photos of Mark, poems he had written, articles about his artwork and documents pertaining to his career as a gifted and celebrated photographer.

In his artist statement, Mark described himself as a "photojournalist of the soul." *Art should express the range of human experience including darkness as well as light, suffering and transcendence, sin and redemption, and doubt as well as faith.* Mark overcame struggles as a learner with dyslexia and graduated with a Masters of Fine Arts from the University of Notre Dame. His work earned numerous awards and was displayed in 15 solo and 26 selected exhibitions nationwide. His art expressed his deep Christian faith and he was known as a creative, compassionate and gentle soul by all who knew him.

Since his death in 2006, two years after Dad's passing, I'd had trouble comprehending how faith survived through such heartrending loss. *Perhaps nothing is more painful than losing a child,* I thought.

Refreshingly, there were no secrets. Arnold and Gloria didn't shy away from my questions. They spoke honestly about the horror, the loss, the anger, *and* the healing. They didn't blame themselves but learned to accept the facts about the disease that had claimed Mark; they found peace through years of prayer, reading, counseling and community support.

"Mark was tired," Arnold said.

Aunt Gloria prepared a simple meal of soup and sandwiches, and before we began eating Uncle Arnold thanked God for his many blessings: for his wife, his son Paul and his partner Sisi, for their three grandchildren, Emma, Walker and Barley, and for our visit.

A few days later when Dave and I were getting into our car, Arnold pulled me close and said, "Keep the faith."

I had rediscovered my people.

———————

In each story I collected, I could see it was the coming together that made the difference. The Germans and Mennonites came together to find a peaceful land to worship and raise their families. The siblings, Carl, Martha, Emma, and Amelia came together to care for each other after their parents had died. The American Indians came together to tell their story in a play as proud people who had survived the Europeans arrival, and fought for their right to stay on their land. My anti-Nazi German relatives came together to offer solace and support to the refugee survivors of the largest genocide in history, breaking ties with family members who participated in the horror. My mother and sister came together to support me, as Dave and I fought to keep our marriage. And as a family, we persevered through the losses of our beloved ones.

As Kimmerer says, "What happens to one, happens to all."

side walks

part 5
summer
returns

The trees act not as individuals, but somehow as a collective.
Exactly how they do this, we don't yet know. But what we
see is the power of unity. What happens to one happens
to us all. We can starve together or feast together.[24]
—Robin Wall Kimmerer

back up north

Dave, the boys and I loved to hike, to locate new and adventurous trials to experience the joy of nature. At times we challenged the boys to make a shelter, or find a life bird (a bird not yet observed), or identify a wildflower, tree or mushroom. So when I found the *Cheboiganing Nature Preserve* in Brutus on Google Maps the family was all in.

On our way, as we passed the Dieterich family farm on Brutus Road, I proudly spoke to the boys about our family history, reminding them to consider putting down their cell phones long enough to remember a time when entertainment involved watching fireflies at dusk and singing songs around a pot-belly stove. They glanced up from their phones and grunted in acknowledgement.

Dave drove a few more miles before turning right into a gravel parking lot. A large sign welcomed us, but as we moved closer, in smaller print under the name of the trail, was a story we'd not heard before. As I began reading, I remembered Aunt Martha saying years ago there had been something called a

[24]Kimmerer, Robin Wall. Braiding Sweetgrass. Milkweed Editions, 2015.

Burn-Out in Brutus. I had not understood what this meant, but reading about it now for myself, I was astounded by what happened.

A National Register of Historic Places sign at the site stated the following:

The Burn-Out, a People Displaced, but not Destroyed: Burt Lake Band of Ottawa and Chippewa Indians (The Cheboiganing Band)

Evidence of many centuries of human settlement can be found throughout the Indian Point and Cheboiganing properties. Studies in the Indian Point Memorial Forest, by Dennis Albert and Leah Minc, in the 1980's, revealed many corn cache pits that had been used by the original human occupants to store their harvests. Pottery fragments estimated to be more than 700 years old have been found, and soil studies revealed charcoal deposits produced by periodic fires set by Native peoples while clearing plots for subsistence agriculture. The Cheboiganing Band of Ottawa and Chippewa Indians, today known as the Burt Lake Band presented the following information of this region's history.

The BLB was a signatory to both the 1836 treaty of Washington and 1855 treaty of Detroit. Through these and similar treaties, tribal nations ceded large tracts of land in the Great Lakes region to the United States in exchange for nominal financial compensation and the continuation of their rights to hunt, fish, and gather on traditional lands. Certain tracts of land, were explicitly excepted from these cessations and reserved for the use of specific tribes including the Cheboiganing Band which was to receive "One tract of 1,000 acres to be located by Chief Chingassanoo or the 'Big Sail' on the Cheboygan River." To this day, the treaty has not been honored and the tribe functions without a reservation of its own.

Beginning in 1850, Band members built at least twenty-one log cabins on their 411 acres of land that "...has been purchased by the said;

Governor of Michigan in Trust for the She boy gan Indians and his successors in office..."

On October 15, 1900, the families of the BLB were unexpectedly and violently ousted from their homes and village on Indian Point by "legalized arson." Cheboygan banker and timber speculator, John McGinn, determined to remove the Native Americans from Indian Point and establish his own claim, obtained tax title to their lands. With the help of Cheboygan County sheriff, Fred Ming, the men, moved from one log house to the next within the traditional Burt Lake Band village, doused each with kerosene and then set them ablaze while ordering everyone immediately off. Some accounts indicate that only the Catholic mission church remained standing. Descendants of this tribe today refer to this incident as the "Burn-Out". The removal violated a trust agreement between the tribe, the State of Michigan, and the U.S. Federal Government. The BLB continues to seek redress for this injustice and has submitted extensive documentation to support its petition for federal reaffirmation.

Following the Burn-Out, many members of the BLB moved from the Point to Indian Trail (today Indian Road) and the surrounding area. Having no money and no place to live, they were taken in by tribal members who already resided on or near Indian Trail...

Today, many tribal members hope to migrate back to their traditional "homelands" which many maps still refer to as "Indianville". The Burt Lake Band continues to operate a tribal office in Brutus which focuses on social, cultural, and economic development. Emphasis on environmental protection, restoration and the preservation and promotion of the native language continue.

(Some information in this publication came from previous document written by Susan Alexander, Amy Colligan, Ruth Flanagan, Melinda Huffman, and Chuck Robbins. Thanks also to Matt Pierie, Kate Tuohy, Rick Wiles, and the Burt Lake Band of Ottawa and Chippewa Indians.)[25]

[25]Cheboiganing Nature Preserve/ Indian Point Memorial Forest. Little Traverse Conservancy, 2024. https://landtrust.org/explore/chaboiganing-preserve-indian-point-memorial-forest/

I was not prepared for this. I felt ashamed and frustrated. Why hadn't I known about this before? All these years coming to Indian River, to Burt Lake, to Brutus. Why had no one ever told me about this horrific event in Michigan history, in the same town where my family had lived for nearly 100 years?

Dave and I gathered Noah and Nate, who were itching to take the hike through the woods, and started into the forest. After a somber hike, we returned to the cottage, where I sat pensively, ruminating about the *Burn-Out*. About the women and children who had been forced out onto the road to watch their homes burn to the ground. About 85-year-old Mary Na-go-mah who walked 30 miles to Cross Village after the *Burn-Out,* where she died the next day. Indian Point, now ironically called Colonial Point, is only six miles by boat from Dave's family cottage, and only six miles from where the Dieterich farm was located.

Six miles. And I had heard nothing. I was determined to learn more. I needed to return to the library in Petoskey.

The library had moved across the street into a large new building. Mary, an accommodating librarian, pointed out the research of Richard Wiles, in a binder entitled: *The Historic Cheboiganing Band of Ottawa and Chippewa Indians, The History of an Unsolved Michigan Mystery-115 Years 1900-2015.*[26] I read through the timeline and let the story sink in, teach and guide me to a path of mourning and thoughtfulness. Wiles stated, *"By 1855, there was a village of 200 or so Odawa located on Burt Lake, with cultivated land, orchards, a large 'sugarbush' (maple grove), two dozen homes (more or less), and a small Catholic Church & rectory. With the exception of livestock, the village held undivided property, including some tools furnished under government treaty."* But because *"Illegal tax assessments lead to illegal tax titles sale"* the Burt Lake Band was stripped, blasted apart, humiliated, robbed of their right to live freely and justly on trust land. Secrets revealed. At the time of the *Burn-Out* Gottlieb and Magdalena had given birth to two children, Carl and Matilda. I'm sure they heard about the horrific circumstances of their neighbors.

---

[26]Wiles, Richard. The Historic Cheboiganing Band of Ottawa and Chippewa Indians, The History of an Unsolved Michigan Mystery-115 Years 1900-2015.

two women

October 14, 1900
Magdalena
Age 25
Husband away logging
Nursed her infant, Matilda
Securely contented in her arms
Nestled under an Heirloom quilt
Rain pattered on the cold window pane
A fire crackled, softly
Lighting primitive walls
Potatoes, corn, apples stored
Logs stacked
Meat and poultry cold packed and preserved
Preparations done
Winter, I am ready
She said with certainty

———————

October 14, 1900
Hattie
Age 26
Husband away for wages earned
Nursed her infant, Maggie
Securely contented in her arms
Nestled under a Native blanket
Rain pattered on the cold window pane
A fire crackled, softly
Lighting primitive walls
Corn, squash, beans stored
Logs stacked
Meat and fish salted and smoked
Preparations done
Winter, I am ready
She said with certainty

October 15, 1900
Cries of terror awaken
Men threaten with righteous indignation
Get Out. This is My Land Now.

side walks

Peeking out a rain-stained window
Neighbors resist
Panic erupts
Bleeding still from birthing
Basket
Baby
Blanket
Out of her home
Accosted by chaos
Kerosene and smoke
Choking, vomiting, stumbling to the street
McGinn and Ming Desecrate
Defile, Destroy, Determined to Take
Land
Orchards
Barns, animals, storehouses
20 Log homes
Hattie wept joining the screaming mothers

Then
She looked down
Upon her daughter's tears
Lifted her chin
And spoke
From a well within
NO!
You destroy my people
Man, you cannot steal our pride
We are Indian
We are Native
We are the First people of this land
Shame on you
Self-indulgent, greed-filled thief
Mother Earth will remember
She will bring us Home

Walking they left
Grandmothers, mothers, children
As she hugged her infant
To her breast
She walked on

side walks

November 1, 1900
Knocking startles
Peering out frost covered window
A woman holds baskets
A baby on her back
Opening the door
Magdalena meets Hattie
Buys two, one for eggs, one for yarn
Offers an empathetic gaze
Thank you
Closes the door
And thinks what she could have said
I'm sorry
I'm so sorry
Please come in and warm up
Under this Heirloom quilt
I can't imagine
How great your loss
And I don't understand
But a part of me does
Because it hurts
When an abusive man
Has the final word.

———————

After the *Burn-Out*, John McGinn moved onto the land. He built a lake home and used the church for his pig-barn. He was never charged for his illegal actions.

Andrew Blackbird, an educated Indian, son of an Ottawa Chief, authored a book entitled *History of the Ottawa and Chippewa Indians of Michigan*. He resided for many years in Harbor Springs as the postmaster, though with very little salary. He had hoped to be a doctor, but was forced to drop out of Eastern Michigan University after two and a half years because funding from the government ceased. Blackbird's poetic lament reminds us of the suffering his people endured.

> *O my destiny, my destiny! How sinks my heart, as I behold my inheritance all in ruins and desolation. Yes, desolation; the land the Great Spirit has given us in which to live, to roam, to hunt, and build our council fires, is no more to behold. Where once so many brave Algonquins and the daughters of the forest danced with joy, danced with gratitude to the Great Spirit for their homes, are no more seen. Our forests are gone, and our game is destroyed. Hills, groves and dales once clad in rich mantle of verdure are stripped. Where is this promised land which the Great Spirit had given to his red children as the perpetual inheritance of their posterity from generation to generation?...The tree that my good spirit had planted for me, where once the pretty brown thrush daily sat with her musical voice, is cut down by the ruthless hands of the white man. 'Tis gone; gone forever and mingled with the dust. Oh my happy little bird, thy warbling songs have ceased, and thy voice shall never again be heard on that beautiful shady tree.*[27]

———————

While researching about the *Burn-Out* at the library, I learned that the Burt Lake Band was hosting a fundraiser. They were raising money for a Traditional Foods Project, a program to offer Band members a chance to reconnect with and reestablish relationships with traditional foods and food

---

[27] Blackbird, Andrew. History of the Ottawa and Chippewa Indians of Michigan. Ypsilanti, Auxiliary of the Women's National Indian Association, 1887.

preparation. Most non-Natives don't realize that with assimilation into white American culture, tribes lost a relationship to the land, their language, and even their traditional meals. The project would introduce new generations to ancient practices, another step in the long journey to come together as a people. At the fundraiser, the Band would be serving two cultural recipes: fry bread with maple butter, and traditional corn soup.

Arriving back at the cottage, I asked Dave if he would like to attend the fundraiser with me. He responded without delay, "Of course. What time?"

The event was held at a roadside park in Pellston, a small town just north of Brutus. Pellston had survived as a viable locality, in large part as a result of the regional airport that made up a large part of the tax base. The park was located adjacent to the old train station, now used as a nascent museum. At the fundraiser welcome tent I bought a T-shirt, and talked to Band members about the medicinal garden they were developing on their land. According to their website, the band was involved in a two-year project that *involves teachings from knowledgeable native instructors about topics such as spear-fishing, making maple syrup, using indigenous plants for food and medicine, and much more.* Their goal is to grow in knowledge, health and well-being.[28] Dave and I chatted with a mother of two children who were attending college. Though American Indians are eligible for significant financial aid from the federal government, these two students had received none since the Cheboiganing Band is not currently a federally recognized tribe. Their land was stolen and the tribal members scattered. The Band is in a paradoxical position: the reason they don't have government standing is in part because their land was stolen and members scattered. The layers of injustice smother hope for recognition.

As Dave and I made our way through the artisan booths, I noticed a handmade quill box for sale made by elder Ken Parkey, with an exquisite Monarch butterfly and pink coneflower. Nola, the director of the Band encouraged me to open it and smell the bark. The scent was spicy, earthy, and reminded me of a walk in the woods. I purchased the box, thrilled to own such a poignant indigenous artifact with its symbol of change: a butterfly emerged from its cocoon.

While paying for our lunch, I met Deborah Richmond, historian of the Burt

---

[28]https://burtlakeband.org/

Lake Band. As Dave was finding a place for us to enjoy our soup, I shared with Deborah about my family who had lived near Indian Point. Just as I was reconstructing my family lineage and story, Deborah was doing the same for the Band, her heritage, and the history of the area since so much had been lost over the years. We were kindred in this way, so we exchanged phone numbers and set up a time to talk.

A few weeks later, Deborah and I connected on the phone. She shared in detail about her family history. Her great-grandmother and white husband owned a "decent-sized farm" on Burt Lake very near the Band's settlement. Deborah's great-grandmother had an older sister who had come from the Upper Peninsula, who married into the tribe at Burt Lake, and was present at the *Burn-Out.* She moved along with the rest of her siblings after the *Burn-Out,* and resettled on Indian Road.

"Growing up we would hear whispers about the *Burn-Out.* The white businessmen wanted the land, so they burned their homes and took it. I never found out more about that till much later." Deborah's grandmother did not pass much down because that older generation had learned to silence their native-side in order to assimilate. "Being Indian was not considered a positive trait," Deborah shared, matter-of-factly. Her grandmother, being half-Indian and half-white, didn't pass down the language or knowledge of their tribal history. "We are always scrambling to learn more. My mother was told as a child when she moved to Lansing not to tell anyone that she was Indian. Can you imagine? It's only now through researching the history that I've learned the details of what happened." She paused. "Do you know Rick Wiles? He's been a treasure. There is no one in our family who has known all the information that Rick has compiled. I am basically in charge of helping our people reconnect with our past. Who is going to teach us? If we want to know, we have to go find it, and re-discover our heritage. It's an interesting way of learning your history."

Deborah continued, "Recently, we were finally given a list of the Indian children who attended the Holy Childhood School of Jesus boarding school. All the tribes have been asking for these records for *years.* The bishop came and presented the book to us at a ceremony. None of my relatives went to boarding school because we were half- Indian and half-white, but most Indian children were forced to attend. A cousin asked to see the book and

Deborah Richmond and Julie
Dieterich Pappas
Photo by David Pappas

Monarch Quill Box
Artist: Ken Parkey. July 7, 2023

found the names of her dad and his siblings, but said *"none of them spoke of it."* I asked my cousin what her grandmother thought and she said, *"I think my grandmother wanted all of them to go because she believed they would get a good education, and she knew they needed to become a part of the American society. But when the kids came back home, they did not talk about things that happened to them, so it was buried. Now we can find out who didn't come home."*

I shared with Deborah the history of my immigrant families, about the Germans and Mennonites who homesteaded the land in Brutus, built log cabins like her family, why they came to the area and how they lived off the land. I thanked her for entrusting me with the heart-breaking yet courageous stories of her people, and we spoke honestly about frustrations and hopes for the future. After a couple hours of sharing with each other, Deborah said, "Miigwech, Giga-waabamin menawaa." (Thank you; See you again.)

After I hung up I reflected on the experiences of Deborah's grandmother. She had been shut down by a society that forced her rich cultural history to fade away, to disappear in the framework of America. Some might call this inclusion. But it was more like erasure. The "great melting pot" sounds innocuous enough when you're in school, unless you were one of those who were "melted" away. No wonder Deborah's grandmother was afraid to share the family stories or tell anyone about her native identity.

The Holy Childhood of Jesus Christ Academy operated from 1829-1983, and has the ignominious distinction of being one of the last boarding schools to close in America. I graduated from eighth grade in 1983. I was angered that in our country — in my lifetime — children were taken away from their mothers and fathers, from the vitalizing culture of their Indian communities. I had walked by that church many times before on visits to picturesque Harbor Springs. But I had no idea that at the boarding school children were mistreated if they spoke in their native Anishinaabemowin language, in some cases even being beaten by the priest or nuns beyond recognition. Several were sexually assaulted.

In *Historic Tales of Michigan Up North*, D. Lawrence Rogers wrote, *Yvonne Keshick, who attended Holy Childhood for eight years, told Emily Fox: "The darker you were, the worse you were treated." Keshick said she was beaten almost every single day. If she got a math problem wrong, the nun would grab her by the head and use her face to erase the math problems on the chalkboard.*[29] But despite the awful mistreatment of some, there were others who benefited from the education, and the opportunity it provided to step out of poverty. This created a challenging dichotomy between the fortunate and the unfortunate, the cared for and the abused.[30]

Survival and scarcity can numb the emotional landscape of the human soul, stripping flesh, breaking bones, forcing victims to put on layers of false-self to cover over debilitating shame. Hurting families bury stories that become secrets; perhaps out of fear that truth will weaken their dignity.

That night I wrote in my journal: I am stronger today knowing the truth. *I commit to pass on the whole story to the next generation, to embolden them to consider a better way. "He has shown you, O mortal, what is good. And what does the Lord require of you? To act justly, and to love mercy, and to walk humbly with your God."*[31]

[29]Rogers, D. Lawrence. Historic Tales of Michigan Up North. The History Press, 2018

[30]https://museumofojibwaculture.net/

[31]New International Version, Old Testament, Micah 6:8

side walks

another way

Justice
Treating fellow
Humans
With dignity
Regardless of fear
Bias
History
Hurt

Mercy
Looking deeply
Past exterior coverings
Meant to preserve
Protect
Offering kindness
Wrapped
In mutual forgiveness
Understanding

Humility
Walking side by side
Arm in arm
Hand in hand
To remember
To recreate
To recognize our value
As created beings
Formed from the dust of the earth
By a good Creator

Build bridges that heal.
Listen with eyes of the heart.
Offer gifts of peace
Seeds of hope
Bandages of comfort

side walks

Together
Opposing power
Of those who
Steal
Strip
Destroy
We stand unified
Dignified
Free of burdens that have
Burned
Bound
Broken

We hope
We heal

into the chapel

I returned to the family cemetery on Red School Road, but was astonished to notice the church Gottlieb and the other settlers had built across the street had disappeared. I assumed it had been torn down. Disappointment flooded my mind; I had hoped to go inside one day. As I glanced up the hill to a sturdy red barn and ranch home just up the road, I saw an open garage door. Being the curious bird that I am, I wondered if they might know anything about the German pioneers in Brutus. Uninvited guests were probably not common for whoever lived here, but I had abandoned any notion of being "common" a while ago. I decided to pay these strangers a visit.

I walked up the long winding driveway, a little anxious, but resolute. No one was in the garage, just a Downy woodpecker fluttering to find its way out. So, I knocked on the front door.

A woman about my age peeked out from behind the door. "Can I help you?"

"Hi. Um. I'm sorry to bother you... but... I'm a.... I'm a relative of one of the German immigrants that homesteaded the land across the street and I wondered... I was wondering if you knew anyone that would have information about them."

She smiled and opened the door a bit more. "Well you might be at the right place. Who are you related to?" she asked.

"I am the granddaughter of Emma Dieterich whose father was Gottlieb Dieterich. He was one of the original settlers."

"You're kidding me! That's amazing," she exclaimed, "*I'm* a relative of the German settlers, too! I am the great-great-granddaughter of John Wurst! He owned land right next to Gottlieb!"

Her name was Dawn Fisher. And just like that I had a new friend. Dawn graciously invited me in and showed me into the living room where I took a seat on her couch. She offered me a slice of peach pie, and we started talking about our common histories. At one point she looked startled — "Wait! Hang on a minute!" She jumped up and hurried out of the room. "I think I might have a photo of your family in front of the log cabin!" Dawn exclaimed from the other room.

I almost peed in my pants.

She called to me from the dining room and asked me to join her. I found her sitting on the floor; Dawn had dug out an old photo album from a stack of keepsakes tucked away in a curio cabinet. Page by page, she showed me photos of the old settlers, and then turned to a page with a family I recognized. I was giddy with joy. She said matter-of-factly, "Yep, I thought I had one! Here is your great-grandfather on his wagon, in front of the old log cabin that was right across the street from where we are sitting right now!"

The photo I had longed to see for over 25 years was on my lap. My eyes welled up with tears, my mouth open in astonishment! "Oh my goodness! Look at that! I have wanted to see this photo for a long-long time! My great-grandfather was a real pioneer! It's really true!" I abruptly took out my cell phone to snap photos of the photo, not wanting to ask her to take it out of its protective plastic cover. Her grandparents had put together the photo album years ago. It lived with Dawn, who had lost both grandparents.

The photo had been taken in 1897. Gottlieb and Magdalena sat in the front seat of a horse-drawn carriage with Carl between them. Bertha, John and Christina were seated in the back. Underneath the photo was a description that read:

> "This picture was taken on the property where Gottlieb and Irene Buchhorn (grandchildren of the Wursts) are now living, 1976. When Gottlieb and Christina Dieterich came to this area in 1883, they had two children, Louise and Mollie, then Bertha, and Christine and John who were twins born 1886. After her death, he married Magdalena and six children were born. He moved from this home to a place east of Brutus where Carl and Martha lived long after their parents died; they were both very active in Zion Evangelical Church which is now U.C.C. (United Church of Christ). Carl was president of the church board several years; Martha was secretary of Women's Guild a long time. All of the children were confirmed in this church and most of them baptized. At one time, Carl was Maple River Township Supervisor."

I asked Dawn what happened to the old church built by the Germans that had been on the land adjacent to the log cabin. She told me it had been relocated to land in Mackinaw City that was in development as an historical museum.

"Are you serious? You mean I could actually go inside?" I asked.
"I'm sure you could. They are open on Sundays!" Dawn replied.

I had found my people.

————————

The following Sunday, I arrived at the *Mackinaw Historical Society's Heritage Village* on a beautifully crisp but sunny Sunday morning. The white chapel silhouetted against a crystal blue sky was the first building I came upon in a collection of structures that had been renovated and relocated to this museum. A docent welcomed me as I announced, a bit louder than necessary, "I'm the great-granddaughter of one of the original German settlers who built this church."

She smiled and said, "Well, you should go right in and look around then." She walked with me to the door and said, "Welcome back, I guess!"

This was the first time, after all those years of peeking in the windows, that I could finally enter the church building where my great-grandparents were married, where my grandmother and her sisters and brothers were baptized and confirmed.

I learned that the building was constructed in 1889 by the original German settlers. According to Irene Buckhorn, a member of the church and grand-daughter of John Wurst, one of the settlers, all sermons and teachings were conducted in German. The chapel was relocated 120 years later to Heritage Village by the Mackinaw Historical Society. After 3 years of elaborate restoration by a team of dedicated conservationists, it was reconsecrated as a house of worship on September 22, 2013. It is presently open to the public and can be rented for special occasions.[32]

I walked through the front doors with a sense of reverence and a deep well of gratitude, under an unpretentious wooden cross. I was the first Dieterich relative in over 60 years to step foot in this spiritual home.

I took a full breath and then another before passing through the vestibule into the sanctuary. Pews handcrafted of sturdy oak guided my gaze forward, row by row, toward the pulpit. A piano to the right and a baptismal font to

---

[32]Mackinaw Area, Historical Society, and Heritage Village, https://www.mackinawhistory.com/

the left stood at attention, church elders ready to deliver grace. Windows along the sides of the spacious corridor allowed enough light to illuminate hymnals without electric light. I walked around alone, contemplative, imagining the families gathering to feast on Scripture each week, the men sitting on the left, the women on the right, receiving encouragement and fortitude for their weekly burdens. These brothers and sisters in Christ travelled many miles through time and place, from Germany to America, through wicked winter winds and hopeful spring rains, through ripe warm summers and peaceful autumn days, through baptisms and burials, confirmations and weddings, through joyous times and hardships. Through it all, they met, persevered, and wove themselves into the fabric of America.

After leaving the museum, I felt profound appreciation to those who funded the move and restoration of this sacred building. As a child I had an innocent faith; I attended Our Shepherd Lutheran School from kindergarten through eighth grade. I knew all the Bible stories. I loved all the hymns, the organ, singing in the choir. I was proud of being a Lutheran. In fact, I was a poster child for my school's brochure. At the Sunday School store where we could cash in commendations for our good work in our Sunday classes, I bought little devotionals the size of a book of matches, and passed them out at neighborhood "studies" I would host, just like my mom who regularly attended Bible studies with her friends. My spiritual zeal even found its way into my play time. When my sister and a friend and I formed a spy gang pretending to eradicate crime from the neighborhood, they took on aliases like Wonder Woman and Isis; I called myself Leviticus. When an older girl in the neighborhood swore during a game of flashlight tag, I proudly stated, "Hey, watch it, I'm a Lutheran!"

I fancied myself a real Christian disciple. A spiritual zealot. A Lutheran's Lutheran. But never in my life did I have to leave my parents, my country, and my way of life to forge a new life.

And yet these are the people who would shape the woman I have become.

———————

Zion Evangelical Church at Heritage Village, Mackinaw Area
Photos by Angie Morthland

into a garden

The next summer, on my way to meet Deborah at the medicinal garden behind the Band's offices, I drove past the family farmhouse and barn. There was a "No Trespassing" sign hanging on a chain strung across the driveway. The land had been purchased by an excavation company that mines for sand. I whispered words of gratitude for my ancestors and drove on.

A little under a mile from my destination, I pulled off the deteriorating asphalt road and parked alongside a small cemetery enclosed by a chain link fence and shaded by hundred-year-old pine and balsam trees. The blue green of Burt Lake shone in the distance.

I got out of my car and took stock of the scene. There were no stone gravestones. Only white wooden crosses. On either side of the cemetery, down winding landscaped driveways, were two massive summer houses, recently built.

I opened the chain link gate and entered the *Cemetery at Indian Point.* This was the location of the *Burn-Out.* The enormity of what had occurred here over a hundred years before sat in my gut, and I tried to reconcile that reality with the beauty and quiet of the place on this warm summer day.

I looked to my right and left. I closed my eyes and took in a deep breath, smelling the pine and balsam, and sighed. Affixed to a large rock a few feet from the gate, was a metal plaque with the names of the deceased Cheboiganing Band of Ottawa and Chippewa Indians who died before the *Burn-Out,* buried on their land before the forced removal. These were Deborah's ancestors. I whispered words of gratitude.

There was a feather lying on the ground. Two Chipping Sparrows defended their nest, and I thought of the voices of the indigenous women who bravely cried out against the injustices and indignities they endured here.

So much pain. So much strength and perseverance.

So much courage.

I paid my respects, prayed for change and turned to leave. A hand-painted wooden, faded blue sign above the exit gate issued a benediction,

"GIVE ME KNOWLEDGE SO I MAY HAVE KINDNESS FOR ALL."

Burt Lake Band Cemetery and Community Garden
Photos by Julie Dieterich Pappas

_____

I turned off the asphalt road, onto a stretch of gravel road, and then onto a beaten path of grass and dirt where I saw the hand-made sign for the Burt Lake Band Community Building and the Band's *Healing Landscape and Three Sisters Garden.* I pulled my car under a lilac bush, and waved at Deborah, who was standing in the garden, about 30 meters away. Deborah looked stately, her hazel-tender eyes emanating warmth and welcome. I grabbed garden gloves and a hand shovel from the hatchback and walked to greet her. "Boozhoo!" *Hello!*

Over the next few hours, we pulled weeds and cultivated the soil together, working our way around the stone path encircling the garden bordered by tree limbs, separated into four sections, each representing a season of life. As we worked, hands in the dirt, sweat on our brow, we spoke honestly about life as women, as friends, as sisters. Sisters whose great-grandmothers lived in this community.

We had come together through the years, over the miles, carried by stories of the past, kneeling on the land, writing a new chapter. Together.

I had found my people.

side walks

side walks

epilogue

During a *Bucket List* trip to Germany, I visited the *Dachau Concentration Camp Memorial Site* where my German cousin assisted the survivors of the holocaust as a Red Cross worker following WWII. No one knew in the town beyond the walls, of the atrocities committed on a daily basis. No one knew. We must never forget.

It was in preparation for this trip, Ann Wilson, a fellow traveler, found the church record of my German relatives as shown below, from the Walterichskirche in Murrhardt, Germany.

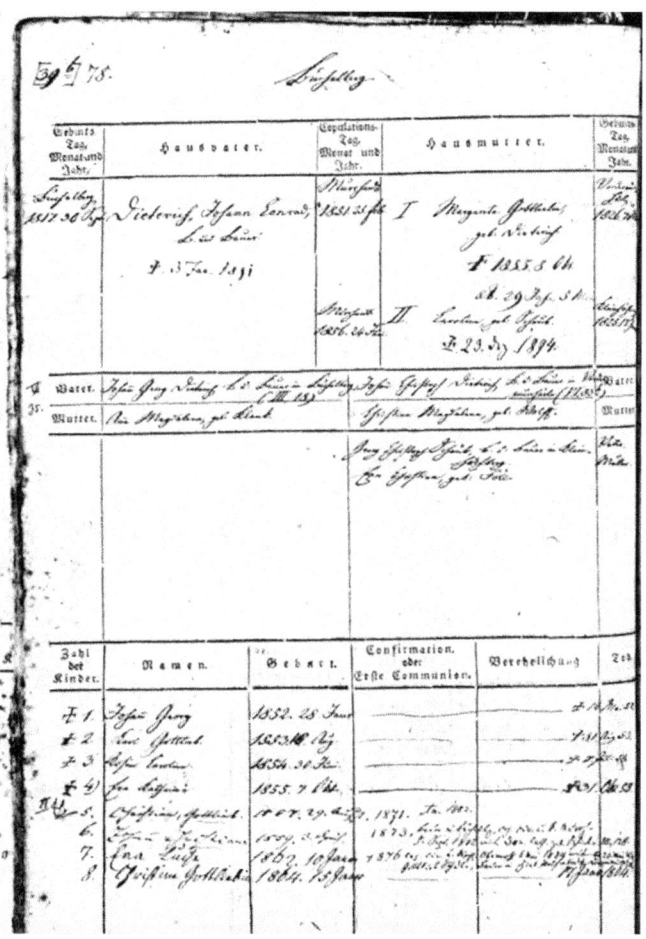

side walks

acknowledgements

Thank you David Pappas, editor, best friend, husband and partner in writing. Your expertise and support have challenged me to keep on, dig deep and write with authenticity and clarity.

Thank you Deborah Richmond, member and historian of the Burt Lake Band, for editing this story, and allowing me to tell part of your own story. You can support the Band's goal to update their headquarters office building and the surrounding landscape by donating on their website at www.burtlakeband.org

Thank you Angie Morthland, president of the board of directors for the Mackinaw Area Historical Society and Heritage Village, for encouraging me to write this story as a descendant of the original builders of Heritage Chapel. You can find more information on visiting and donating to this comprehensive historical and educational community project at www.mackinawhistory.com

Thank you Renée Tanner, graphic designer and owner of *Eyes on Design,* for your work on this publication. It was a thrill to unexpectedly discover our familial connection as 3rd cousins, and great-great-granddaughters of John Kilmer during the worst ice storm of the century in Petoskey, MI.

Thank you Dr. Froese at Anderson University for kindly translating the German letters.

Thank you Richard Wiles, for your passionate work in writing and publishing the story of the Burt Lake Band in your book "A Cloud Over the Land", available at www.burtlakeband.org

Thank you Greenwood Cemetery for accessible archives on your website www.gwood.us

Thank you Maurice Eby, for publishing a comprehensive history of the town of Brutus. Obtain a free copy of "The History of Brutus and Maple River Township" at: https://www.emmet.migenweb.org/resources/brutus_history_maurice_eby.pdf

Thank you Nate Pappas and Laura Isaacs for your striking photography.

Thank you Aunt Martha, Aunt Mitzy, Gary Hilpert, Johanna Hilpert, Edgar

Hilpert and Arnold Hilpert for sharing your time and memories as shared in this book.

A percentage of the proceeds of this book go directly to the Burt Lake Band as they promote the preservation of their Chippewa and Ottawa culture and the legacy of their people through education, community events, and the *Traditional Foods Project*. Proceeds also benefit the Mackinaw Historical Society and Heritage Village for their continued work on persevering the legacy of families who have shared the land and made history in northern Michigan.

museums to visit

- Museum of Ojibwa Culture at Old Mission Saint-Ignace, www.museumofojibweculture.net
- Andrew J. Blackbird Museum on East Main Street in Harbor Springs
- The History Center of Cheboygan County where you'll see a Native American Log Cabin, one of three that survived the *Burn-Out*

Deborah and Barbara Richmond stand in front of one of the cabins restored from the Burn-Out at the History Center of Cheboygan County in their traditional ribbon skirts.

Photo by Julie Dieterich Pappas

side walks